A Closer Look at
GUIDED READING

A Closer Look at GUIDED READING

David Hornsby

ELEANOR CURTAIN
PUBLISHING

First published in 2000
Eleanor Curtain Publishing
906 Malvern Road
Armadale Vic 3143
Australia

ISBN 1 875327 55 X

Production by Publishing Solutions
Edited by Ruth Siems
Designed by David Constable
Printed in Australia

Acknowledgments

The author would like to acknowledge the following people for reading the manuscript of this book and providing valuable feedback.

Classroom teachers and curriculum coordinators: Mary McDonald (Findon PS, Melbourne); Jo-Ann Parry and Carol Braybrook (Ringwood Heights PS, Melbourne); Debbie Sukarna (Dyatmika School, Bali)

Reading Recover tutors: Leonie Wigney (Melbourne); Julie Zrna (Mildura, Australia)

Teacher educators: Professor Marie Emmitt (Deakin University, Melbourne); Janet Evans (Literacy Consultant, Liverpool, England); Robyn Platt (Literacy Consultant, Australia; ELIC tutor trainer, USA), Jan Senior (Literacy Consultant, Darwin)

Thanks are also due to the following for permission to use copyright material:

Stenhouse Publishers for fig. 4.2 and extract on p.70 from *Apprenticeships in Literacy: Transition across Reading and Writing* by Linda J. Dorn, Cathy French & Tammy Jones. Copyright © 1998. Reprinted with permission of Stenhouse Publishers; Mimosa Publications for *A Zoo* by Andrea Butler, *What Has Spots?* by Jackie Goodyear, *Just Like Grandpa* by Cheryle Semple and Judy Tuer, *Too Much Noise* retold by Brenda Parkes, *The Lonely Giant* by Lucy Lawrence, *The Monster of Mirror Mountain* by Roger Vaughn Carr © Mimosa Publications: available in the UK from Kingscourt Publishing, in Australia from Rigby Heinemann, in New Zealand from Shortland Publications, in the US from Rigby Education; Mondo Publishing for *Zoo-Looking* by Mem Fox. Text © 1996, 1998 by Mem Fox; illustrations © 1996 by Mondo Publishing; Heinemann for fig. 1.2 adapted by permission of Constance Weaver: *Reading Process and Practice: From Sociolinguistics to Whole Language*, 2nd edn (Heinemann, A division of Reed Elsevier Inc., Portsmouth NH, 1994), and fig 1.8 reprinted by permission of Lynn K Rhodes and Curt Dudley-Marling: *Readings and Writers with a Difference: A Holistic approach to Teaching Struggling Readers and Writers*, 2nd edn (Heinemann, A division of Reed Elsevier Inc., Portsmouth NH, 1996); Macmillan for *Baby Elephant's Sneeze* written by Sandra Iverson, illustrated by Jan van der Voo © 1996 Sandra Iverson, *The Fierce Old Woman Who Lived in the Cosy Cave* written by Virginia King, illustrated by Sarah Farman © 1995 Virginia King, Reproduced by permission of Macmillan Education Australia.

Contents

Introduction

This book is about guided reading. I wouldn't write a book about guided reading if I didn't believe it was a powerful teaching procedure that helped children to use reading strategies effectively. But we need to remember that guided reading is only one strand of a balanced literacy program. In this introduction, I want to remind you that our reading programs are only successful if they lead children to be independent readers for life. We want the children leaving our schools *choosing* to read; not just able to read. We want them to have a *passion* for reading.

What is success?

Would teachers, school systems and governments invest their time, expertise, energy and resources teaching children to fly and helping them achieve their flying licences if we never intended them to become pilots? Of course not. Then why should we invest so much time and energy, and spend so much money on literacy programs if we don't intend children to become readers? The criterion for success of a literacy program is surely that children become **independent readers** who **choose** to read for many different purposes throughout their lives.

Children learn to read and *choose* to read when reading programs are based on beliefs such as those summarised below.

- We *intend* that all children will become readers. Our attitude is most important. We show the students that *we* are readers and we demonstrate an unshakeable belief that they *will* learn to read.
- We insist on using books that have meaning and we continually reinforce the fact that reading for meaning has our top priority. We are aware that we need books that not only help children learn to read, but also read to learn. We understand that, for learning to read, there is power in reading to learn.
- We use a wide range of authentic texts in various formats. We understand the power of literature and its potential to passionately engage children in their transactions with text. We understand the interest and influence of non-fiction, and the appeal of everyday, mass-media texts.

- We know about reading. We know what constitutes development in reading and we know the signposts that indicate development along the way.
- We understand that we help children when they enter a 'reading apprenticeship' with the teacher. In the resulting partnership, the teacher interacts with children in daily literacy events that take the apprentices from beginner, to novice, to experienced reader.
- At every developmental stage, we provide maximum support when children are reading challenging texts that are difficult for them, some support when the texts have a balance of supports and challenges, and little or no support when the texts are simple for them. We understand the 'gradual release of responsibility' model and use it to help us provide the optimum amount of support for the reading apprentices in our classrooms.
- We use books that provide their own reward – books that children respond to in many different ways. We don't rely on bribes such as stars or marks or stamps. Children will read books when the books themselves are worthwhile.
- We appreciate that children learn to read because they are given daily opportunities to *read*. During classroom reading time, we ensure that children are actually reading, and not spending inappropriate amounts of time engaged in activities that are *related* to reading. We also ensure that there are many purposeful reading practices in our classrooms so that children read to achieve other things.

These beliefs, or their implications, underpin the rest of this book.

The power of literature

This book is about one strand of your reading program: the guided reading strand. Guided reading is a powerful way of helping children to develop their reading skills and strategies, and it should be an important strand of every reading program. Nevertheless, we must remember that guided reading is a means to an end. It is one of the means we use to help children become **independent readers for life**. Once they are independent readers, what do we want them to read? We want them to read all kinds of texts, for all kinds of purposes. We want them to read for entertainment and pleasure; for information and realisation; for the love of the language itself. We certainly want them to read for daily survival. The texts they may need to read to fulfil all these purposes will vary enormously. They might include picture story books, traditional stories, contemporary stories, fantasy, plays, poetry, newspapers, magazines, train timetables, children's own writing, biographies, information reports, instructions, classified advertisements, public documents, electronic mail, and so on. We would certainly insist that their reading diet would include classical and modern literature of a wide variety.

For guided reading, we mostly use texts that are short enough to be read in one session. Even with the self-extending and experienced readers (see chapter 1), we use texts that are complete in themselves, and which can be read in one guided reading session.

Given that our goal is for all children to become ***independent readers for life***, we need to keep guided reading in perspective. Yes, guided reading is a powerful teaching procedure and is relevant for all children. Yes, we must use every effective procedure known to us in order to help all children become independent readers. But I have been concerned by the numbers of teachers who have felt pressured by the policies of education departments to take on this procedure or that strategy, this form of organisation or that structure, even to the detriment of other effective strategies. Sometimes, the baby has been drowned in the policy bath water.

While I have been fortunate to have opportunities to work with teachers and children in several countries, and to help them implement guided reading procedures in their classrooms, I have been unhappy to hear so many make comments such as:

'Now that we have to do guided reading every day, we don't have time for our literature program.' (a teacher in Melbourne, Australia)

'Literature just won't fit into our literacy hour.' (a teacher in London)

'Literature is devalued now. Today, we only hear about text level, sentence level, and word level!' (a teacher in Liverpool, England)

'We're only supposed to use decodable texts now. Everything has become so mechanical, and the emphasis on test scores forces us to focus on skills to the detriment of the love of reading.' (a teacher in California, USA)

'The emphasis is on mechanical skills now, not literary skills.' (a teacher in Florida, USA)

'The data-driven mania makes us think that policy makers think we are teaching robots rather than human beings with hearts and emotions.' (a teacher in Melbourne, Australia)

'We're always being told about the *skills* of reading, and how they should be taught and tested. They've forgotten about what it is to be fully literate in today's world.' (a teacher in Colorado, USA)

And most telling of all, Peter Benn, a non-teacher friend, saw some of my panic when the deadline for the manuscript of this book was getting close. He asked me what I was writing about, and I described guided reading as well as I could to a non-teacher friend. Later, I received an e-mail message from Peter, in which he recalled the wonders of the literature he read during his school days in the 1950s and 1960s in Australia. I paraphrase some of his message here:

> How poor I would have been without the wonderful thoughts, ideas, and images I received through literature … Imagine the world without the adventures of Pooh Bear and his friends, or the planning and scheming of the three billy goats when they were confronted by the troll … I can't even imagine a world without a mouse called Mickey, who never has a harsh word for anyone. He just giggles and shrugs off adversity … There is no shortage of good literature. But when are most children going to hear it and read it and love it if they don't have a diet of it in the classroom? They all deserve the touch of happiness in their hearts that literature can give them. Praise be to those human beings who fiddled with drawing pencils, and wrote a few words from their hearts. They have made our world a place with less fear, and some hope for universal love and understanding. … Now write *your* words so that you encourage teachers to carry the torch that won't die out.

What a command to heed!

Programs with passion

The words from my non-teacher friend had a powerful impact, and reminded me that **passion** is just as important as any **program.** We need both. We need texts that have been written by passionate authors, and teachers who are passionate about reading and learning to read. We also need programs that reflect our current understandings; programs that are based on the beliefs outlined above. Careful programming brings order to our literacy curriculum and ensures that it is balanced, cohesive and inclusive. But when we inject our programs with passion, we have a much greater probability of helping children become independent readers who **choose** to read for life.

There is a huge body of research (not just from education, but from psychology, neurology and other disciplines) which reminds us of the essential and inextricable link between cognition and emotion. In his book *Reading Lessons: The Debate over Literacy*, Gerard Coles argues that 'reading educators who want to craft an education that can successfully serve all children, must make the role of emotions a primary concern.'

Emotional response can improve or inhibit cognition and learning, and yet the 'hot topics' in reading education today do not show a concern with the affective. (See Cassidy & Wenrich 1998/1990.)

Mem Fox (1996) also reminds us that we cannot separate the cognitive from the affective. Questions about the texts and the methods are not the only questions; an essential question is, *What happens between the teacher and the child?* We need teachers who are readers themselves, who love literature, and who inject their programs with passion.

I am excited by our increasing knowledge of how children learn to read. I am enthusiastic for programs that have a balance of complementary teaching procedures that reflect our current understandings. I am constantly amazed by teachers' efforts to continue their professional development and by the many extra hours they devote to their students.

Along with Peter Benn and all non-educators, along with all those who are passionate about reading, I would plead that we don't lose sight of our major goal. Maintain your passion for reading, for sharing authentic texts with children, for helping children become life-long readers.

Some useful references for using literature in the classroom are provided in 'Further reading'.

CHAPTER I

Learning to read

What is reading?

Theories of reading

Up to the 1960s, research into reading looked mainly at the visible print system or surface features of language. Since the 1960s, research has broadened and included studies of the linguistic, cognitive and social systems that are essential to learning to read. Moustafa (1997) refers to the resultant 'groan zone' – the transitional time when our old beliefs are being challenged by new understandings. The old common-sense or 'person on the street' view was based on observable reading behaviours and the visible surface features of our written language. Research over the last few decades has been able to go beyond those things we can observe on the surface, and delve into the 'invisible' linguistic, cognitive and social systems.

This recent research has led to different theories of the reading process being formulated, all of which add to our understanding. Some of the theories are noted here, but it is not the intention of this book to describe them. There are many excellent reference books that do so.

In his psycholinguistic theory of reading, Goodman (1967, 1979, 1984) describes reading as a process in which we deal with information and construct meaning continuously. We make predictions, confirm or reject these predictions as we read, self-correct when meaning is disturbed, and integrate information from the text with our current knowledge to comprehend the text.

In her transactional theory, Rosenblatt (1978, 1985, 1988) describes how we bring all our experiences, including our cultural experiences, to the reading process. She refers to the transaction that occurs between the reader and the text, and reminds us that the meanings we make depend on our experience and background knowledge.

Smith (1975, 1988) has helped us to understand that the more non-visual information we have when we are reading, the easier it is to process the visual information (print) in front of us. He argues convincingly that as readers, we need more than the ability to use phonics rules and pronounce words correctly. Since his theory draws on an understanding of the social nature of reading, and from the disciplines of psychology and linguistics, it is referred to as a socio-psycholinguistic theory.

Others have also drawn our attention to the fact that reading is a social practice, and that the ability to use and understand language for different purposes is crucial in our society. The concept of 'critical literacy' developed during the late 1980s and has been the subject of much attention during the 1990s. The table below, drawn from Lo Bianco & Freebody (1992) and Luke & Freebody (1999), describes four different 'families of practices'. The practices range from code-breaking to the ability to analyse a text as a 'crafted object' which has been designed to 'position' readers in a certain way. When readers apply text-analysis practices, they recognise the author's attempts to persuade them to a point of view, they recognise stereotypical treatments of characters, they appreciate that different interpretations of the same text are possible, and they understand that texts are not neutral. In other words, they are 'reading-thinking' critically.

Practices	What the reader actually does
code-breaker	understands and applies knowledge of the 'technology' of written script (ie the relationship between spoken sounds and the ways they are represented as written symbols)
text-participant	draws on and applies knowledge of the topic, text structure and syntax to make sense of a text
text-user	draws on knowledge of the role of written texts within the society in order to use them to participate in social activities in which texts play a central part
text-analyst	draws on awareness that all written texts are crafted objects; is able to read text 'critically'; understands how the text is 'positioning' the reader

Figure 1.1 Four 'families of practices'

Luke & Freebody (1999) use the term 'family of practices' to indicate that the practices are 'dynamic, being redeveloped, recombined and articulated in relation to each other on an ongoing basis.'(p. 6) They emphasise that '*all* of these repertoires are variously mixed and orchestrated in proficient reading and writing.' (p. 7, my emphasis)

Theories of learning

Theories of learning in general have also broadened over the last few decades. Since the 1960s, researchers in linguistics, psychology and education also helped us to understand that in all learning, children are *active* contributors. They don't just passively absorb what is around them. They interact with their environment and engage in complex formulation and re-formulation of hypotheses as they develop meaning for the realities and the signs and symbols around them. The predominant model of learning before the 1960s was based largely on behavioural psychology and is referred to as the *transmission model of learning*. It is characterised by drilling skills, memorising facts, and habit formation. Lessons from a pre-determined program are taught and tested in a definite order or sequence, and the emphasis is on discovering children's weaknesses. The model that has most support from educators is known as the *transactional model of learning*. The transactional model is based on the knowledge that humans fundamentally construct their own knowledge. It is characterised by hypothesis formation, use of errors to make further hypotheses, teaching that responds to learners' needs, and building on the learners' strengths. As Weaver (1994) points out, the constructivist concept of learning permeates reform efforts in every major curriculum area.

The transmission and transactional models are at opposite ends of a continuum. Figure 1.2 compares the two models of learning in general, with some points about learning to read in particular.

Which model?

Marie Clay defines reading as 'a meaning-getting, problem-solving activity which increases in power and flexibility the more it is practised.' (Clay 1991, p. 6) She has difficulty accepting the transmission view that reading is an exact process of seeing and saying words (p.14).

Clay points out that reading is a problem-solving process in which the reader samples the print to search for meaning. She goes on to say: 'It is difficult to see how one could avoid forming hypotheses in an activity like reading which is both perceptual and cognitive.' (p. 14) It is the *transactional model* that recognises the reader's search for meaning. Readers construct meaning through the formulation and re-formulation of hypotheses as they sample the print and use many different strategies to attend to information from different sources.

Both models would accept that reading is made up of many component skills, strategies and behaviours. In a final analysis, there may be little disagreement on what has to be learned. However, a major difference between the two models is related to the order in which the skills,

Transmission model	Transaction model
Common-sense view of person-on-the-street who sees only surface structure of text and directly observable reading behaviours	Informed view of professional with understandings of deep structure of language, and knowledge of reading strategies inferred from observable behaviours
Bottom-up processing: smallest units to biggest units (letters to words to sentences)	Two-way processing: whole to part to whole; multi-directional transactions between the whole and the parts
Reading proceeds from surface to deep structure; from what's on the page to what's in our heads. Meaning comes from the text to the reader.	Reading proceeds from deep to surface structure; from what's in our heads to what's on the page. Reader takes meaning to the text in order to get meaning from it.
Reductionist Behavioural psychology	Constructivist Cognitive psychology
Habit formation; avoiding mistakes prevents formation of bad habits	Hypothesis formation; errors necessary for encouraging more sophisticated hypotheses
Students passively practise skills, memorise facts	Students actively pursue learning and construct knowledge
Direct teaching of pre-packaged, pre-determined curriculum	Responsive teaching to meet learners' needs and interests
Taskmaster, with emphasis on cycle of teach, practice/apply/memorise, test	Mastercraftsperson, mentor: emphasis on demonstrating, inviting, discussing, affirming, facilitating, collaborating, observing, supporting
Lessons taught, practised and/or applied, then tested	Mini-lessons taught as demonstration, invitation
Reading materials characterised by unnaturally stilted 'basalese' language	Reading materials include a wide variety of materials in natural language patterns
Performance on decontextualised tests is taken as a measure of learning of limited information	Assessment from a variety of contextualised learning experiences captures diverse aspects of learning
Learning is expected to be uniform, same for everyone; uniform means of assessment guarantee that many will fail, in significant ways	Learning is expected to be individual, different for everyone; flexible and multiple means of assessment guarantee all will succeed, in differing ways
Adds up to a failure-oriented model, ferreting out the learners' weaknesses	Adds up to a success-oriented model, emphasising the learners' strengths

Figure 1.2 Ends of the transmission–transaction continuum
(adapted from Weaver 1994, fig. 9.1)

strategies and behaviours are learned. In other words, the contentious issues involve the **when** and **how** questions.

Reading programs based on the transmission model would suggest that there is a specific, pre-determined order, and that learning is uniform for everyone. Clay makes the following significant remark:

> One reason to value the current advocacy for 'whole language' approaches to literacy instruction is because they do not try to control which sources of information in a text the child shall learn first. They do not prevent the child's exposure to any aspect of the task. (1991, p. 17)

However, teachers whose practice is guided by a transactional model must have finely tuned observation and assessment procedures in place to ensure that they know 'what cues in texts (or sources of information) individual children are attending to and whether children are moving forward.' (Clay 1991, p. 17) This is certainly a challenge they must address. The guided reading procedure helps because it is not only a powerful teaching procedure, it is also a powerful assessment procedure and will help you to monitor which cues individual children are attending to, and whether they are moving forward or not.

From apprentice to expert

Reading apprenticeship

We know that we help children move forward and learn to read when they enter a 'reading apprenticeship' with the teacher. In *Apprenticeship in Literacy*, Dorn, French and Jones (1998) view children as apprentices in learning. They borrowed this concept from Rogoff (1990). Children, as apprentices in learning, 'acquire a diverse collection of skills and knowledge under the guidance and support of more knowledgeable persons'.

In the partnership between the teacher and the children, the teacher (more knowledgeable partner) intercedes to ensure that children (apprentices) engage in daily literacy events that take them from beginner, to novice, to experienced reader.

The literacy club

The apprenticeship view parallels Smith's description of how children learn to read by joining the 'literacy club' (Smith, 1988). Children join the club as apprentices, but graduate as independent readers. They start as beginners, but the teacher reads to them and provides many other reading demonstrations through many other literacy events each day. The children become involved in reading with the teacher, asking questions, and getting help along the way. The teacher plans specific instruction with the intention of addressing specific needs so that the apprentices take more and more responsibility for the task. The teacher gradually releases responsibility with the expectation that the learners take more control (see 'A model of instruction' p. 21).

Working in the zone of proximal development

To get from the beginning apprentice level to the expert level, we help children most by supporting them as they operate at the level which is just beyond what they can do without assistance.

Vygotsky (1978) refers to the zone between a child's actual developmental level and the potential developmental level with adult support as the zone of proximal development. When you provide support for children within their zone of proximal development, they are in a very powerful learning situation.

The most significant learning occurs within this zone of proximal development. In guided reading, you give the apprentice readers a text they cannot read independently, but one with challenges they can overcome when supported by your interactions with them. (Other strands of your literacy program will generally occur within this zone of proximal development too. For example, in shared reading, you will use more difficult texts than those used in guided reading, but you will also provide more support. The level of support varies with the degree of difficulty of the text.)

When you are helping children within the zone of proximal development, it is essential to provide multiple, explicit demonstrations. As apprentices, children are also actively involved in reading; they learn to read by reading. There are continual demonstration–engagement interactions, with the teacher being informed by feedback from the children so that the level of support is always being fine tuned. The teacher demonstrates with a teaching–learning intention, but adapts the level of support

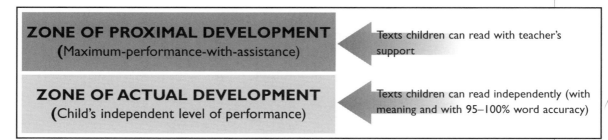

ZONE OF PROXIMAL DEVELOPMENT
(Maximum-performance-with-assistance)
Texts children can read with teacher's support

ZONE OF ACTUAL DEVELOPMENT
(Child's independent level of performance)
Texts children can read independently (with meaning and with 95–100% word accuracy)

Figure 1.3 The zone of proximal development and reading

to that which is required for participation and independent processing by the children.

Because the interactions between you and the children are constantly being fine tuned according to the way in which the children are processing the information, it is not possible to write definitive notes on how a particular book will be used for guided reading with a group of children. Teaching notes can only suggest *one possibility* or a 'best guess' at how the interactions will proceed. The notes provided in chapter 3 suggest possibilities only. They are provided as a model to stimulate your thinking, not to give you a set procedure.

Rather than teaching notes for guided reading, we need teachers who have an understanding of learning theory, an understanding of the reading process and the developmental stages of reading, insights into the children's strengths and needs, and a knowledge of the texts to be used. Nothing takes the place of teachers with strong professional knowledge and commitment to children's learning.

Taking control: from other-regulatory to self-regulatory behaviour

When you view the acquisition of literacy as an apprenticeship between an expert reader and one who is learning to read, you intend that the learner becomes more and more capable of taking control of the reading strategies and becomes a 'self-monitoring' reader. We want children to become consciously aware of the reading strategies so that they can pause, reflect, consider options, and take control of their own reading. We want them to 'know what they know'. As this happens, they depend less on the need for others to regulate their reading behaviour, and turn more and more to self-regulatory behaviour.

In her outstanding book *Children's Minds* (1978), Margaret Donaldson helps us to understand that children achieve the conscious awareness they need as they interact with others in the various literacy events that occur. During these literacy events in the classroom, teachers use explicit demonstrations, they talk about the demonstrations, and they use explicit language about language so that the children acquire greater understanding about literacy concepts and greater awareness of what it is they need to do to read. The greater their awareness, the greater their control.

Donaldson argues that the manner of teaching, or methodology, is influential:

> Once the teaching of reading is begun, the manner in which it is taught may be of far-reaching significance ... the *process* of becoming literate can have

marked – but commonly unsuspected – effects on the growth of the mind. It can do this by encouraging highly important forms of intellectual self-aware-ness and self-control. (p. 97)

In other words, methods are not neutral. Methods carry messages: they tell the children what you consider to be important. Methods inhibit or promote growth of the mind.

Obviously, the transaction model of learning, with its emphasis on

- construction of meaning
- hypothesis formation and use of errors to encourage more sophisti-cated hypotheses
- responsive teaching which seeks student feedback and includes demonstration, invitation, discussion and support
- use of natural language texts
- and individual pathways through predictable patterns of development

will provide more of the conditions for encouraging self-awareness and self-control than the transmission model.

If a child learns skills without understanding, Vygotsky would main-tain that 'he has not mastered the system but is, on the contrary, bound by it' (quoted in Donaldson 1978, p. 99). To apply this to an example from reading, if a child learns about the graphophonic system through a series of predetermined, sequenced skills lessons, he may well be bound by that knowledge, rather than served by it. We hear evidence of this when children painfully plod through printed text, trying to sound out every word as they go. We see it in children who have patterns of miscues where visual information has been used to the exclusion of semantic and syntactic information, with the result that meaning has been destroyed.

'The hope, then, is that reading can be taught in such a way as greatly to enhance the child's reflective awareness, not only of language as a symbolic system but of the processes of his own mind.' (Donaldson 1978, p. 99) Guided reading has the potential do to this very powerfully.

The place of directive instruction

There are implications for the place of instruction and the type of instruc-tion that is appropriate in order to help children move from apprentice to expert reader.

One of the major differences between the transmission model and the transaction model is this very issue of instruction. A transmission model is characterised by direct instruction from a predetermined curriculum, assuming that learning will be uniform for everyone. In the light of what has already been discussed, we would have to reject direct instruction.

And any look at the history of our classrooms also tells us that direct instruction doesn't work.

Extremes on either side of a continuum tend to be misleading. The issues are also clouded by narrow use of terminology, or negligence in defining what is meant, or both. For example, some holding an extreme view of the transactional model might be heard saying, 'I don't teach. I demonstrate, invite, discuss, affirm, facilitate, collaborate, observe, support' and so on. I would argue that teaching is all those things – and more! Why would that teacher say, in effect, 'I don't teach'?

Weaver et al (1996) make a distinction between *direct* instruction and *directive* instruction. They describe direct instruction as the kind which is typically prescribed in the lesson plans of prepackaged programs. The following points are made in comparison:

- directive instruction is relevant instruction offered at the point of need
- directive instruction can include direct instruction
- directive instruction implies guidance and support, or scaffolding, not merely the transmission of information
- learners do not necessarily need directive instruction to learn something
- different learners need varying amounts of directive instruction
- learners may benefit from directive instruction at different points in their learning

Guided reading provides many opportunities for this kind of relevant directive instruction.

A theory-driven balanced approach

The appropriateness of the term 'balanced' has sometimes been questioned, but it is entirely appropriate in the context discussed by Strickland (1998).

> Avoiding instructional extremes is at the heart of providing a balanced program of reading instruction. However, finding the balance should not imply that there is a specific balanced approach. Nor should it suggest a sampling method in which 'a little of this and a little of that' are mixed together to form a disparate grouping of approaches euphemistically termed 'eclectic.' Ultimately, instruction must be informed by how children learn and how they can best be taught. Achieving informed balance is an ongoing endeavor that requires knowledge, time, and thoughtfulness. (p. 52)

When teachers understand the principles of teaching and learning, when they understand what reading is, and when they have a knowledge of what constitutes development in reading, then the kind of eclectic approach referred to above is anathema. A 'bits and pieces' approach will not do. Everything you do to facilitate children's learning is informed by your professional knowledge and experience. This knowledge and experience helps you to develop a theory of how children learn in general, and how they learn to read in particular. When you have a well-developed theory, based on knowledge and experience (not ignorance or prejudice) then you **teach with intention**. Everything you do is coordinated to assist learning. This teaching/learning theory is behind your planning, your program, and your practice. Without such a theory, teachers can only deliver a so-called 'bits and pieces' curriculum, taking children down different paths, causing confusion, and leaving children to compensate for the inevitable holes in the program. Unfortunately, only some children adequately compensate for those holes; others are left in the dark.

Predictable patterns but individual pathways

Developmental stages in reading

Harste, Woodward & Burke (1984) argue convincingly that there are no developmental stages in literacy. The reading and writing strategies that literate adults use are the same as those used by beginning readers and writers. Children do not learn one set of strategies when they start school, abandon those and learn another set when they are promoted the next year, abandon those and learn another set the following year, and so on until they become literate. The strategies do not change, but through experience, readers fine tune the strategies and learn to use them in increasingly coordinated ways. 'The process children engage in is not a pseudo form of the "real" process; it *is* that process.' (p. 69) **There is a continuum of more and more sophisticated reading, not discrete stages.** However, at certain times in their schooling, most children do exhibit specific behaviours, understandings and attitudes that tend to 'cluster' into what we might call 'bands' or 'stages'. While well-defined stages do not exist, it is useful for **teachers** to understand something of the clusters of behaviours, understandings and attitudes so that they are able to observe and assess children more carefully and thereby make more appropriate decisions about the teaching/learning opportunities that present themselves.

Weaver (1994) refers to *recurring patterns* in literacy development. Even though they are mental constructs that don't exist in reality, they help us understand 'how children gradually construct their own understanding of reading …' (p. 77) She warns that 'the day-to-day, child-by-child reality of literacy development is much messier and less clear-cut.'

In his book on literacy assessment, Johnston (1997) also reminds us that the development of literacy is not linear: '...the order in which literate knowledge is acquired and whether something is higher order or basic is more of our own making than not.' (p. 138) And further: 'Literacy development is not a simple journey along a straight and narrow path. One reason for this is the complexity of literacy. Development occurs along many dimensions at once, and on different dimensions in different circumstances. For this reason alone, we should expect irregular, nonlinear patterns of literacy development.'

But Johnston goes on to say: 'Although literacy development is generally somewhat uneven, there are certain areas of predictability.' (p. 143) In other words, ***there are predictable patterns or trends, but individual pathways***. The individual pathways that children take should not prevent us from recording their development. Since reading development is complex, irregular and nonlinear, it is not possible to record it with numbers or letters or grades. Rather, we map each child's development through sophisticated assessment procedures such as those discussed briefly in chapter 3.

Every child is always ready to learn more

When you understand what constitutes development in reading, and when you have effective observation and assessment procedures, you can look for the developmental signposts that indicate something about the pathways that children take. When you provide the support they need to make further progress along their pathways, they are all ready to learn more. Good teachers support the participation of every single child. A good reading program is flexible enough so that all children are ready to learn more. (Johnston 1997, p. 140)

Naming the stages

The practice of helping teachers by clustering behaviours, understandings and attitudes into 'bands' or 'stages' has been adopted by educational authorities worldwide. However, different terminology for the stages is used in the official curriculum documents that teachers are expected to follow, so the way in which you describe the developmental stages may vary. Common terminology includes:

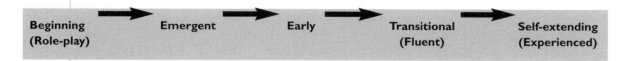

| Beginning (Role-play) | → | Emergent | → | Early | → | Transitional (Fluent) | → | Self-extending (Experienced) |

Beyond the self-extending (experienced) stage, we might refer to the *advanced* stage.

The terminology you use will depend on your setting, and the official curriculum documents used in your part of the world. You may find the following references useful for understanding more about the developmental stages.

- Fountas & Pinnell (1996, p. 178) describe emergent, early, transitional and self-extending stages
- Don Holdaway (1990) describes a development of reading skills in the appendix to his influential book *Independence in Reading*
- Margaret Mooney (1988, pp. 8–11) describes the typical reading attitudes, understandings and behaviours at each of the emergent, early and fluency (transitional) stages
- Education Department of Western Australia (1997), *First Steps*, Melbourne: Rigby Heinemann

Clay (NZ)		emergent	early	fluent		
Fountas & Pinnell (USA)		emergent	early	transitional	self-extending	
Western Australia (*First Steps*)	role-play	experimental	early	conventional	advanced	
Terminology used in this book	beginning	emergent	early	transitional	self-extending	advanced

Figure 1.4 Terminology used to name the stages. Note: There is no attempt to 'align' these stages. 'Early' in one continuum may not be exactly the same as 'early' in another. However, there is considerable overlap.

Labels used in this book	Possible age ranges*	Possible grade range	Reading Recovery levels used	Vic: Early Literacy (Previously Keys to Life)	WA: First Steps
Beginning (guided reading not appropriate at this stage)	3.0–5.5	Pre-school to middle Prep or Reception	n/a	Beginning	Role play
Emergent (guided reading starts here)	4.5–6.5	Pre-school to early Year 1	1–5 or 6	Emergent	Experimental
Early	5.0–7.0	Prep (Reception) to late Year 1	6–11 or 12	Early	Early
Transitional (Fluent)	6.0–8.0	Early Year 1 to early Year 3	12–17 or 18	Fluent	Conventional
Self-extending	7.5–10	Mid Year 2 to late Year 3	18 +		
Advanced		Mid Year 3 to late Year 4+	Beyond Reading Recovery levels		Advanced

Figure 1.5 Comparison of stages for Australia

* We see very young children (age 3 and less) who exhibit some of the characteristics of the 'beginning' reader. For example, they like to look at texts as they are read to them, they know where a story starts, and they demonstrate reading-like behaviours as they role-play' reading. Some may even read familiar texts, relying heavily on memory and use of illustrations. Sadly, however, for a variety of reasons, some children will still be learning these things at age 6. While most children will show characteristics of the developmental stages within the age ranges shown in the table, some children will reach these stages at even earlier ages than indicated, and some at later ages. The range shown will, however, cover most children.

Labels used in this book	Possible age ranges	Reading recovery levels used	Bands/SAT levels	National Curriculum level	Suggested colour coding
Beginning	3.5–5.5	Guided reading not appropriate at this stage			
Emergent	4.5–6.0	1, 2 3, 4, 5	Bands 1 2	Working towards Level 1	Pink Red
Early	5.0–7.0	6, 7, 8 9, 10, 11 12, 13, –	3 4 5	Working within Level 1	Yellow Blue Green
Transitional (Fluent)	6.0– 8.0	– 13, 14 15, 16 17, 18	6 7	Working towards Level 2	Orange Turquoise
Self-extending	7.0–9.0	19, 20 21, 22	SAT Levels 2C 2B	Working within Level 2	Purple Gold
Advanced	8.0–10+	23, 24	2A	Working towards Level 3	White

Figure 1.6 Comparison of stages for England

BEGINNING READERS are learning how texts work, where a story starts and finishes and which way the print proceeds.

They like to look at texts and have texts read to them.
They are developing an understanding that thoughts can be represented by print.
They demonstrate reading-like behaviours as they reconstruct texts and role-play reading.
They read some known texts, relying heavily on memory and the use of illustrations.
They are often able to dictate text which they can recall and read to others.
They respond to and discuss texts, relating what they know about the world and their
  own experiences to the ideas, events and information in the texts.

EMERGENT READERS are learning that a text is a consistent way of telling a story or of relating information.

They understand that the words convey a constant message.
They use illustrations to help them understand the text.
They can usually match written words to spoken words.
They are developing knowledge of sound-letter relationships.
They are beginning to experiment with reading and take risks when reading simple texts.
They read much of the familiar print in the classroom and school environment.
They express personal views about a character's actions.
They are able to retell the sequence of events (or ideas) and are able to make connec-
  tions between events (or ideas).
They are developing an understanding of the concepts of letter, word, sentence.
They are developing a sight vocabulary of the most commonly used words (can read
  many in context, and some in isolation).
They can recognise and extend alliteration and rhyme.
They are using semantic cues, syntactic cues, and some graphophonic cues.
They are beginning to read familiar texts with fluency and expression.

EARLY READERS are becoming more confident in using a variety of strategies for using semantic, syntactic, and graphophonic cues.

They are able to adapt their reading to different types of texts.
They recognise many words, and are willing to take risks on new texts.
They are establishing the habit of reading for meaning.
They are establishing the habit of self-correcting when meaning is lost.
They can use details from the text to support their retelling of fiction or discussion of
  non-fiction.
They can identify initial, medial and final sounds in words.
They can use familiar words to help them work out new words.
They are beginning to 'read punctuation' so that their oral reading is phrased and fluent.

TRANSITIONAL READERS, or fluent readers, competently integrate all cue sources to make meaning.

They see reading as purposeful and automatic.
They have established ability to make connections between what they know and under-
  stand, and what is new.
They relate the meaning of the text to their own experiences and knowledge to confirm
  or challenge the content.
They read a variety of texts and can predict or self-correct to make meaning.

Figure 1.7 Developmental stages in reading (adapted from *Teaching Readers in the Early Years*, Keys To Life Program, Department of Education, Victoria, Australia & Longman, 1997)

A model of instruction

The 'gradual release of responsibility' model

A model of instruction developed by Pearson and Gallagher (1983), called the gradual release of responsibility (GRR) model, was adapted by Rhodes and Dudley-Marling (1996) as shown in figure 1.8. The adaptation provides a strong philosophical base for literacy events that occur throughout the school day, and provides a rationale for the well-known '*to, with and by*' continuum (see figure 1.9).

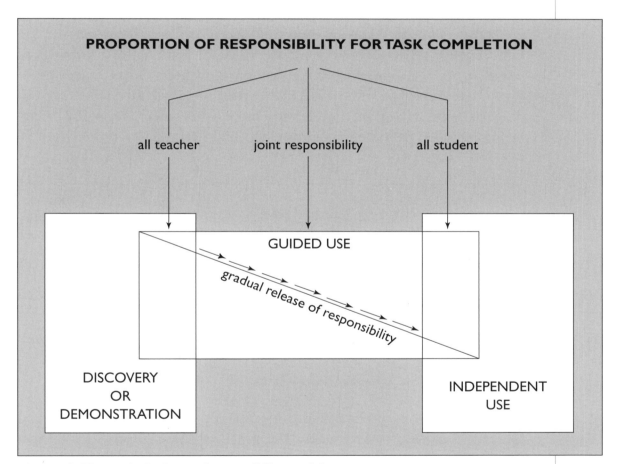

Figure 1.8 The gradual release of responsibility model
(from Rhodes Dudley-Marling 1996, fig. 2.9)

Providing support

At *every* developmental stage, we provide different levels of support. We provide maximum support when we read *to* children, different levels of support when we are reading *with* children, and little or no support when children are reading independently *by* themselves. As Figure 1.9 shows, we provide:

- total support when we read to children
- a great deal of support when children are reading challenging texts that are difficult for them
- some support when the texts provide some challenges, but lots of support as well, and
- little or no support when children are reading texts which are easy for them to read independently

In other words, we put the 'gradual release of responsibility' model into operation.

The art of teaching is knowing how to shift along the continuum shown in figure 1.9. If we provide too much support when it *isn't* needed, we are taking away opportunities for learning. If we provide too little support when it *is* needed, we frustrate learning. We know how much support to provide when we have well-developed theories of learning and teaching, and models that help us to put these theories into practice. Some important theories and models have been discussed briefly in this chapter; the references provided will lead you to further professional reading.

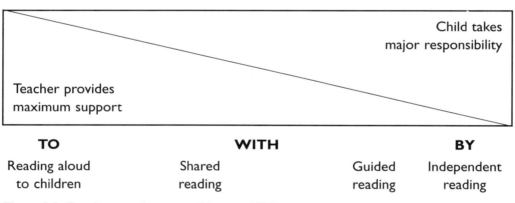

TO	**WITH**		**BY**
Reading aloud to children	Shared reading	Guided reading	Independent reading

Figure 1.9 Continuum of support (Mooney 1988)

At **every** developmental stage we use texts that cover a wide range of levels and genres, or text types. The range of levels is provided so that the 'apprentices' gain experience using reading skills and strategies in different ways. For example, with easy text they will be able to practise orchestrating the reading skills and strategies in coordinated ways. With challenging text, they will benefit from the teacher's support and will, among other things, see how to apply a known strategy to overcome a challenge in the text.

CHAPTER 2

Guided reading in a comprehensive literacy program

A multi-strand program

The 'to–with–by' continuum

The 'to, with, by' continuum shown in figure 1.9 can be extended to show where all components of a comprehensive literacy program fit.

By reading *to* the children, you are providing maximum support and helping the children to experience what it is to be literate. At the other end of the reading continuum, you expect children to take major responsibility and to read *by* themselves. In modelled writing, you provide maximum support by. composing the text, putting it on paper, and talking about it. The children are free to witness the act of writing – to see what it is to be a writer. At the other end of the writing continuum, you expect children to write *by* themselves, or independently. Figure 2.1 shows the continuum, identifies the components of a comprehensive program, and shows where those components are placed on the continuum. Figure 2.2 summarises each of these components.

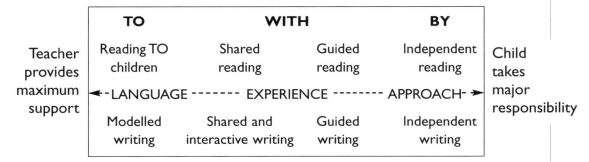

	TO	**WITH**		**BY**	
Teacher provides maximum support	Reading TO children	Shared reading	Guided reading	Independent reading	Child takes major responsibility
	◄-LANGUAGE ------- EXPERIENCE ------- APPROACH-►				
	Modelled writing	Shared and interactive writing	Guided writing	Independent writing	

Figure 2.1 An extended version of the continuum of support (adapted from original concept by Margaret Mooney)

Links between the components

All the strands or components of a comprehensive program are interdependent and support each other. Each component depends upon, and contributes to, every other component.

> The components are 'linked together in two powerful ways:
> - through the ***oral language*** that surrounds, supports, and extends all activities
> - by the ***content*** or topic of focus
>   (Fountas & Pinnell 1996, p.21, emphasis added)

Oral language is involved in every aspect of the reading/writing program, but it is also used throughout the day to develop and extend meaning, to question, to inform, to play with ideas, to express feelings and reactions, to state and restate tentative understandings, to explain. In every part of the curriculum, and certainly across all the strands of a comprehensive literacy program, oral language is used to learn and to relearn. At the same time as children are using language to learn, they are learning the language, and learning about the language (Halliday 1973).

Content is provided through the topics of the texts themselves. A unifying topic or theme will be particularly important for the read-aloud, shared reading, independent reading and language-experience components; it will only be indirectly important to the guided reading strand of your program. The books used for guided reading are separate from those used for the rest of the program. If the content of a guided reading book happens to be related to the content of other work you are doing in your program, that is a 'happy accident' rather than a planned intention. Nevertheless, if you are doing a unit of work on families, it might be appropriate to choose *Just Like Grandpa* for guided reading for one of your groups, but only if it is at the appropriate level to match their needs.

For reading aloud, shared reading and language-experience, it is often possible to choose texts that support units of work in other areas of curriculum. For example, if you are doing a unit of work on farm animals, you may decide to use *Mrs Wishy-washy* for shared reading with the whole class. So curriculum areas related to the study of society, science and the environment often provide the content for children's speaking, listening, reading and writing. Topics from the content areas provide interest and act as powerful unifying themes. They create 'an overarching web of meaning that helps children connect the various reading and writing activities in a purposeful way.' (Fountas & Pinnell 1996, p. 25) These ideas are further discussed in *Planning Curriculum Connections: Whole School Planning for Integrated Curriculum* (Murdoch & Hornsby 1997).

However, 'stand-alone' literacy units can also provide this kind of unifying theme. The following list gives an indication of some of the possibilities:

- author studies (for example: Mem Fox, the Grimm Brothers, Cynthia Rylant, Margaret Wild, Charlotte Zolotow)
- author–illustrator studies (for example: Pamela Allen, Chris Van Allsburg, Jeannie Baker, Byrd Baylor, Anthony Browne, John Burningham, Eric Carle, Tomi de Paola, Pat Hutchins, Ezra Jack Keats, Leo Lionni, Beatrix Potter, Maurice Sendak, Tony Ross)
- illustrator studies (for example: Marcia Brown, Terry Denton, Anne James, Pamela Lofts, Patricia Mullins, Peter Parnall, Craig Smith, Julie Vivas)
- studies of single titles
- studies of concepts such as time, prejudice, personal journeys, independence, and survival through realistic fiction
- stereotypes about the elderly in realistic fiction
- male/female roles in traditional literature compared with male/female roles in contemporary literature
- nursery rhymes and contemporary rhymes
- folk tales of a particular country
- modern retellings of folk tales
- Aboriginal myths and legends
- Aesop's fables, contemporary fables
- tall stories
- family stories, adventure stories, animal stories
- animal fantasy stories (for example: the Just-So stories, the Paddington Bear stories, *Runaway Ralph*, *Charlotte's Web*, *One Hundred and One Dalmations*)
- free verse, concrete poetry, narrative poetry, humorous verse
- 'peculiar people' (for example: Mrs Pepperpot, Pippi Longstocking, the Borrowers, Thumbelina, Imelda in *The Story of Imelda, Who Was Small*, Aunt Sponge and Aunt Spiker in *James and the Giant Peach*, Treehorn in *The Shrinking of Treehorn*)

The list of possibilities for 'stand-alone' literacy units goes on and on. All provide the unifying links between the various strands or components of your literacy program. This approach to planning (through integrated content units and through 'stand-alone' language units) is further discussed in *Planning for English* (Sukarna, Hornsby & Jennings 1996).

An overview of all components

The following table provides an overview of all the components of a comprehensive reading and writing program. All are interdependent and support each other.

Component	Description	Supports & challenges
Reading to children	Read to children daily, several times a day. More than anything else, reading to children stimulates their desire to become a reader. Some teachers find that it helps to provide an appropriate climate (and secures the children's attention) if they do something special. For example, you might use a special 'reader's chair', or you might light a candle during read aloud time. Plan what you read to children, so that you cover a wide variety of different texts over time.	Major challenges in the text
Shared reading	Shared reading encourages all children to participate in reading. Favourite texts are read and reread. All cooperate to build meaning for the text. Individuals participate at different levels. As the text becomes more familiar, children take more control over the reading, and the teacher explicitly demonstrates and teaches reading strategies. The children learn to articulate the strategies as they explain what they do to read. Once the text is quite familiar, it is used to teach specific skills at the word and letter levels.	A balance of supports and challenges in the text
Guided reading	Guided reading provides an opportunity for small groups of children within the same developmental reading stage to apply strategies they already know to texts they do not know. The texts are carefully matched to the children so that they can apply their strategies to overcome the challenges in the text and read it independently, with success. Guided reading allows children to show how they manage a text on the first reading.	Many supports in the text, but some challenges
Independent reading	Independent reading provides time for children to enjoy reading a text without the need for assistance. Time should be planned for independent reading by all the children every day, but children should also have many other opportunities to choose to read throughout the day. During the planned, silent reading time every day, the teacher must also be reading. (Many children may never see an adult reading.) Opportunities for independent reading help children to 'catch the reading habit'. The children will have access to a wide variety of reading materials.	Text provides many supports

Component	Description	Supports & challenges
Modelled writing	The teacher composes and writes down the text. The children observe, respond and question. As the teacher composes and writes the text, he or she 'thinks aloud' to help the children understand the process.	Maximum support from the teacher
Shared and interactive writing	In shared writing the children work together (whole class or groups) to compose a text. The teacher, as a member of the group, may contribute to the text and help to guide the way in which the text is constructed. The teacher scribes for the children so that they can focus on composing the text. Interactive writing is a form of shared writing. However, the teacher sometimes hands the pen over to a child and asks that child to write the next word, or the first letter of the next word, or whatever is appropriate. ie. a 'shared pen' technique is used.	Shared and interactive writing
Guided writing	Guided writing can be managed in two different ways. Each approach has a different main purpose. (1) One or two sessions may be planned for small groups of children who need assistance with specific writing skills. (2) Many sessions, building upon shared reading and writing of a particular genre, are planned. Firstly, the children are immersed in the genre during reading. Secondly, they compose a text in that genre during shared/interactive writing. Finally, they are guided to write their own text in that genre.	Children take responsibility for writing, but with teacher support
Independent writing	Independent writing must be a daily component of the writing program. Children need opportunities to choose to write for a variety of purposes and a range of audiences. They need opportunities to enjoy writing about their own topics and for their own purposes. Opportunities for independent writing help children to 'catch the writing habit'. The children will have access to a wide variety of writing materials.	Children challenged to attend to aspects all writing
Language experience	The class shares an experience and the children are given opportunities to express their understandings of that experience, or to respond to it, through talk, drama, art/craft, music. The experience, and the children's responses, are used (with groups) to generate an oral text that is dictated to the teacher and written down as a 'wall story'. The text is reproduced in individual booklets for each of the children in the group. The text is used for study of conventions (such as punctuation, spelling, vocabulary).	Support from shared experience, oral language base, and teacher

Figure 2.2 Components of a comprehensive literacy program

Reading to children

It is absolutely essential to read to children every day. Many studies have shown that children who were read to before starting school became the best readers (Clark 1976; Durkin 1966; Krashen 1993; Teale 1984; Thorndike 1973; Wells 1986). When you read to children, they learn to love reading, and you demonstrate the pleasures and rewards of reading. However, you also demonstrate the *nature* of reading.

When you read to children, they learn:

- how narratives work (story structure or 'story grammar')
- how other genres work (information books, recipes, explanations, etc)
- how different genres use different language (for example, narrative texts use personal pronouns; reports or procedures generally do not)
- that certain genres have special language features (for example, narrative uses expressions such as *once upon a time, lived happily ever after, in the deep dark woods*, and features such as alliteration, assonance and rhyme)
- that different forms of a genre exist (for example, narrative includes folk tales, legends, tall stories, parables, etc)
- that their own experiences and understandings help them to comprehend

When you read to children:

- they hear stories they are unable to read for themselves
- they want to write their own texts
- they make predictions about what is to come and they practise many other important reading strategies
- they develop a 'literacy set' (Holdaway 1979) which includes a knowledge of the concepts about print (where to begin, which way to go)
- they learn about things they could not experience themselves
- they increase their vocabulary and develop broader concepts

By reading to children, you introduce them to new authors, new illustrators, new forms of text. You make them more aware of the wonderful opportunities to experience adventure, humour, family life, and you help them to participate vicariously in all kinds of life events. You help them to know what it is like to be a sports star, or what it is like to go into space. You help them to imagine worlds they would never dream about. You help them to know what you can learn from books and to discover that there is a whole world of information at their fingertips. In other words, you give them purposes for life-long reading.

If the children in our classrooms don't have purposes for reading, then none of the other components of our program will make sense.

Shared reading

For shared reading, all the children need to be able to see a copy of the text being read. Consequently, big books are often used for shared reading. However, you can also use a text on an overhead projector, or multiple copies of a book with a group of children. It can be shared reading as long as all the children participating can see a copy of the text. The text can be available commercially, but it could also be the text resulting from shared or interactive writing, or language-experience.

In shared reading, you (the 'master reader') guide the children as they (the 'apprentices') read with you. In shared reading, you all work together to construct meaning for the text. In a mixed-ability group, different children bring different expertise. Some of the children may have good word analysis skills; others may have relevant and important semantic knowledge to bring to the text. Together, they work cooperatively to continue building meaning.

When you first introduce the text, you provide maximum support. You may even read most of the text, but you will have the children making predictions along the way. You will help them to develop the sense of story and comment on character's actions, setting, and so on. When revisiting the text for other shared reading sessions on following days, you will expect the children to take more responsibility for reading more of the text without your help. (See Davidson, Isherwood & Tucker 1989; Dorn, Fisher & Fisher-Medvic 2000; French & Jones 1998; Holdaway 1979; Lynch 1987.)

The shared reading procedure follows the four steps or phases that Holdaway describes in his learning model:
- demonstration (the teacher reading the book)
- guided participation during rereadings
- individual reading and, finally
- performance (individual children reading the text aloud to others)

Obviously, the levels of teacher support required will vary according to the year level, and the kind of text you are using with the group. As the children become more confident during rereadings, shared reading is used to help the children learn more complex skills. Dorn et al describe the use of a pointer, framing cards, masking questions, cloze procedures, sentence strips and word cards to help the children with relevant problem-solving.

In shared reading, skills are learned in the context of meaningful, familiar text. The children are actually engaging with the text and reading. They are tackling the text with a problem-solving attitude and learning or using skills; they are not practising skills in isolation.

An important purpose of shared reading is the explicit demonstration of reading strategies, and the articulation of what those strategies are. Gradually, you expect the children to articulate the strategies, and to explain what they are doing as they read. You will prompt them with questions such as: *How did you know that? How did you work out that word? What could you do now? How could you check that? Why did you think that word was …?* All these questions are asked in order to get the children to articulate the reading strategies for themselves. (See page 32.) So in shared reading, we ***teach*** the reading strategies; in guided reading we expect children to ***use*** the strategies they already know. Obviously then, a priority at the beginning of the year is to get your shared reading program underway.

	Shared reading	**Guided reading**
Emergent and early stages	Focuses on **teaching** the reading strategies	Focuses on **using** the reading strategies
Transitional (fluent) and self-extending stages	Continues to focus on reading strategies, but now gives more attention to: character, plot, setting, style, mood; form of text, text structure, language features; information	Attends to coordination of all the strategies over longer texts; but now includes attention to: character, plot, setting, style, mood; form of text, text structure, language features; information

Figure 2.3 Some differences between shared and guided reading

Guided reading

A nutshell statement

In guided reading, you work with a small group of children who are at the same developmental stage of reading. You select an unknown or unfamiliar book that provides just the right balance of supports and challenges so that the children can read most of it independently. The children are reminded to use reading strategies to problem-solve as they read for meaning.

> In guided reading, the teacher helps the children to use strategies they *already* know so that they are able to read an unfamiliar text independently, with success.

Let's look at each part of this nutshell statement.

• 'the teacher helps the children to use strategies …'

As the teacher, you focus on helping the children use ***reading strategies*** to read for meaning. The reading strategies are meaning-making strategies, so meaning is always an intentional outcome. Figure 2.4 gives a list of common reading strategies. It is not a finite list of course, because all the strategies are overlapping and 'networked'. Some of the strategies listed could be combined and described as one strategy; others could be broken down into several component strategies. The list should not be read as a definitive list, but it will help you to think consciously about the major strategies and to keep them in the foreground of the children's thinking. You might like to photocopy figure 2.4 and keep it with you as you teach. You may also wish to consider making a large chart with the heading 'Our reading strategies'. As you discuss and use reading strategies during shared reading and language-experience activities, you can have the children help you to write them up on the chart. It's a good idea to write the strategies in 'child-friendly' terms. For example, you could start the list with: 'It helps us when we're reading if we …' The chart can then be used as a reference during guided reading sessions.

• 'strategies they *already* know …'

Your questions and prompts are used to remind children to use the ***strategies they already know*** to work out what they don't know. They learn the strategies mainly through shared reading and language-experience. It's during shared reading and language-experience that you demonstrate and talk about the strategies, over and over again. You also expect the children to talk about the strategies, and question them in ways that require them to articulate what they are doing. Unfortunately, many children can only articulate one reading strategy: 'I try to sound it out.' We are happy that they can articulate that strategy, because it *is* a strategy that sometimes helps. However, we want children to have a wide range of problem-solving strategies for reading, and to be able to articulate ***all*** of them.

• '…to read an unfamiliar text independently, with success.'

Guided reading lets children demonstrate their use of strategies on the *first reading* of a text. An aim of guided reading is to have the children read most of the new text independently. However, you may sometimes read some of the text to the children to get them into it, or to help them hear common or repeated syntactic structures. You will read only as much text as necessary to enable the children to take over and read independently. Most of the reading will be silent reading (see pp. 86–90). In fact, guided reading has been described as 'reading silently under the teacher's guidance'.

Talking-thinking-reading through text

Guided reading is often described as a methodology which helps children to 'talk, think and read' their way through a text (Mooney 1995). As the teacher, you help the children to engage with the text, to predict their way through it, to check and confirm their predictions, and to self-correct when necessary.

Margaret Mooney (1994) describes guided reading as a time of 'trying and exploring' and 'initiating and controlling'. Children explore reading strategies which, in turn, leads them to take control of the reading process and accept responsibility for reading with meaning.

> … you show the children how to find resources within themselves and within the book to gain and maintain meaning for and by themselves…'
> (p. 7)

Guided reading is a procedure for the ***first reading*** of a text. The children may revisit the text on following days for important but different purposes. It is important follow up to guided reading, but the intentions are now different.

Strategic reading

One of the aims of our reading program is that children become *strategic readers*. We want them to be **aware** of what they are doing when they read, how they solve reading problems that arise, and what they can do when they're 'stuck'. The more strategies they have, the more possibilities there are for problem-solving.

When we are reading text which is easy for us, we are generally not consciously aware of the strategies we are using. However, when a challenge in the text confronts us, we will often be forced to consciously consider which strategies to employ. The strategies we use will be influenced by our purpose for reading, any situational constraints (such as the need to read something in a given time) and by our understanding of the reading problem confronting us.

As children problem-solve their way through a text, you can ask the kinds of questions that help the children to become conscious of their strategy use. They then see how strategies help them and they come to value those strategies. Also, they are now able to monitor their strategy use more effectively. They are strategic readers. As Peter Johnston says, being strategic 'is much better than just having strategies'. (1997, p.124)

Being strategic is much better than just having strategies.

Having a wide repertoire of strategies is essential, but Johnston cautions us that strategies are useless if they are not used in the context of the child's purposes and feelings. 'The last thing we need are classrooms full of students who are able to check off all the strategies on a checklist but who never pick up a book or a pen.' (p. 129) We still want children to choose to read. We must attend to their hearts as well as their minds.

Some typical reading strategies:

1 Uses background knowledge

2 Uses context to make predictions

3 While reading, confirms, modifies or rejects predictions

4 Monitors own reading by asking questions such as: Does it *make sense*? Does it *sound* right?

5 Uses graphophonic cues

6 Asks: Does it *look* right?

7 Recognises miscues that disrupt meaning

8 Self-corrects miscues that disrupt meaning

9 Uses pictorial cues

10 Rereads or looks back

11 Reads ahead

12 Rereads text before an unknown word, then beyond the unknown word, before focusing on print details within the word

13 Searches for specific information

14 Cross-checks information

15 Uses one-to-one matching and other location skills to find specific print

16 Asks for help

Figure 2.4 Typical reading strategies

Shared reading	Guided reading
Read BEYOND the text; interpret text in relation to the children's experiences.	Read INTO the text; help children use strategies they know; help them attend to print.
Focus on MEANING; develop meaning by ensuring that there is a transaction between the author's and children's experiences, emotions, thoughts, insights, knowledge.	Focus on STRATEGIES. The reading strategies are meaning-making strategies; they require children to attend to meaning.
Most of the reading is ORAL. Predictions about following text may be made; predictions will be confirmed or rejected as reading continues.	Most of the reading is SILENT. Teacher 'cues children in' (eg 'Read page x with your eyes to find out who/what/ … so-and-so did/saw …'
TEACHER is prepared to do most of the reading; children are encouraged to 'come in and out of the reading' as they can. Some children in the group will read the text with the teacher; others will read little of the text on their own but will be attending to the text and learning.	CHILDREN do most of the reading. At the emergent and early stages the teacher may read part of the text so children can pick up rhyme, rhythm, language patterns etc. They can then make predictions based on what they have already heard.
Will read both NEW, unfamiliar texts and FAMILIAR texts. Shared reading of a new text will have different purposes from shared reading of familiar texts. Each time a text is 're-visited', the teacher will have a new (or additional) purpose.	Will generally be NEW, unseen text (we want children to test their reading strategies on unfamiliar text; we want them to make predictions, check them, and either confirm or reject them). Guided reading of familiar texts will have different purposes.
Will usually be a MIXED ABILITY group. The children work cooperatively to develop meaning for the text.	Will usually be a SIMILAR ABILITY group. Each child helps to read the text independently.

Figure 2.5 Some differences between shared and guided reading

Independent reading

The research is clear: opportunities for daily, independent reading result in higher levels of comprehension and better levels of reading achievement overall. (Allington 1983; Anderson Wilson & Fielding 1988; Fielding & Pearson1994; Krashen 1993; Pearson 1993).

Just plain reading has been shown to improve student's comprehension, even as measured on standardised tests. (Pearson 1993, p. 507)

During independent reading, we give children opportunities to apply reading strategies to self-chosen books. Many of the books from which they choose will be easier than the books used for instructional purposes, although a wide range at different levels of difficulty will be available. Sometimes, the choices are limited. For example, at the beginning of a new school year, when you don't yet know the children very well, it is wise to select books *you* know, and to have the children choose from those. Sometimes, you will select books that support a unit of work in science or social studies, and ask children to choose from those. Sometimes, you will provide books that support a language unit (fantasy, stereotypes in text, an author study, etc) and the children will have to choose from those. So there is always choice, but sometimes the choice is constrained so that other curriculum goals are met.

Sometimes, the children will be allowed to read with partners, but it is preferable to have them become more and more experienced with independent, solitary reading. The actual act of reading is quite solitary, but we respond to reading in social and shared ways. After sustained silent reading, you need to provide the necessary environment for shared response and enjoyment.

Very young children may like to read aloud to each other, but we want children to learn to read silently (or at least quietly) at an early stage. Many *would* be able to read silently – it's just that nobody told them that they could actually do so. Before school, and when they first start school, many of the reading demonstrations involve adult readers reading aloud. Consequently, most young children learn that reading is something you must do with your mouth. We need to help them understand that they can read with their eyes and their brain. During the later stages of shared reading, when a text is very familiar, you can ask school beginners to 'read this part quietly with your eyes'. Do it with a sense of fun and it even becomes a game for them to cover their mouths with their hands and then read with their eyes.

Young children love to read with a partner, but it can still be silent reading. For example, you could teach them the 'say something' strategy. Each child in the pair reads the same section of text silently, at the same time. After reading the section, child A says something about it to child B. They then read the next section of text silently, but this time, child B says something about it to child A. They continue in this way, alternating until the book is finished. (The section of text could be one page, a double page, or any other convenient section.)

During independent reading time, children will be allowed to do lots of easy reading. They will read familiar books, or new books which are several levels lower than their instructional level. Clay reminds us that when children are allowed to reread familiar text, 'they are being allowed to learn to be readers'. Furthermore, she adds that 'the orchestration of complex [reading] behaviours cannot be achieved on a hard book … Returning to easy reading is one way of developing the smooth orchestration of all those behaviours necessary for effective reading.' (1991, p. 184).

Independent reading promotes
- the ability to choose books wisely
- awareness of different purposes for reading
- sustained reading
- the independent use of strategies for a wide range of texts
- enjoyment of reading
- a sense of calm

Lots of easy reading promotes
- confidence
- the ability to make predictions
- fluent orchestration of reading behaviours
- expressive oral reading
- awareness of text structure
- independent problem-solving
- further enjoyment of reading

Allington & Cunningham (1996) agree that children need lots of easy reading. 'When children struggle with the material they are reading, they cannot apply the strategies that good readers use and do not develop the habits and attitudes that good readers do.' (p. 53).

Independent reading and the reading habit

Allington and Cunningham make the point in chapter 6 of their book *Schools That Work: Where All Children Read and Write* (1996) that time matters in teaching and learning literacy. They argue that some schools need to reorganise their day to increase the amount of time devoted to the teaching and learning of literacy. They also argue that teachers need significant blocks of time with *all* their students together. Obviously, what teachers do with that time is critical, but they *must* have the time.

There is much significant research supporting what common sense would tell us: the more time we spend on literacy, the more literate children become. Likewise, the more time we provide for children to actually read independently, the more likely it is that they will catch 'the reading habit'.

The language-experience approach

The language-experience approach was first associated with people such as Russell Stauffer (1970), Roach Van Allen (1976) and Maryann Hall (1976) in the United States. They were concerned mainly with language experience as an approach to help children learn to read. The language-experience approach incorporated more aspects of the writing program when the 'process writing movement' influenced our thinking in the 1980s. Van Allen reminds us that the approach is based on ideas and concepts 'rooted in antiquity'. The ideas are not new. He summarises the concepts in the following way:

> I can think about what I have experienced and imagined.
> I can talk about what I think about.
> What I can talk about I can express in some other form.
> Anything I record I can recall through speaking or reading.
> I can read what I can write by myself and what others write for me to read.
> As I write, I represent the sounds I make through speech, and I use the same letters and letter patterns over and over.

You start with the language and the experiences of the children themselves. Sometimes individual experiences are used as a basis for the procedure, but more commonly, whole class shared experiences form the starting point. These shared experiences may be planned or spontaneous.

Planned experiences may include	and *may* be linked to
- hatching chickens	- a science unit on life cycles
- making a chocolate cake	- a unit on humorous poetry, including Shel Silverstein's 'Chocolate Cake'
- role-playing family situations	- a social studies unit on families
- viewing a film	- a language unit on fantasy
- visiting local shops	- an environmental unit on packaging

Spontaneous events can also be wonderful starting points. They often capture the children's interest and engage them powerfully. For example, when a lawn mower threw a stone through our classroom window, we talked about safety issues, occupations (a glazier came to replace the glass), the properties of different materials (glass, putty) and the use of certain tools. This was after we had all calmed ourselves down after the shock of crashing glass. The event, the fright we got, the repair of the window, and all the associated activity, were shared experiences which generated much language for the literacy program.

The following is an outline of a typical language-experience approach:

1. Sharing and discussing an experience (interacting with others, telling, illustrating, responding to what others say and write).
2. Listening to stories, or other forms of text, related to the experience (taking on board what others have to say and relating it to your own experience).
3. Expressing the experience in other ways (through drama, music, drawing, painting, making models, writing).
4. Telling (composing) your own oral text about the experience and then dictating it for the teacher to scribe on to a large chart. Revising the written text (often referred to as a 'wall story') until it captures the intended aspect of the shared experience. (Note that a 'wall story' is rarely a 'story'; it is more commonly a retelling, an explanatory text, a procedural text, a report, or other form of text).
5. Making a booklet of the 'story' for reading and sharing.
6. Using the text for sequencing, cloze activities, study of punctuation, etc.
7. Returning to the text for vocabulary work, study of common spelling patterns, study of graphophonic relationships, and other skills.

Through this procedure, the children are able to use their own knowledge and experience to construct a text. The text, based on the oral language generated by the experience, provides maximum support for these learners.

The text generated through a language-experience approach is the kind of text that Clay (1991) calls a *transition* text. Transition texts are written texts that are closely related to the child's oral language. They include language-experience texts, but also the 'natural language' texts which have been written to closely match children's oral language. It is essential to supplement literary texts with these transition texts if we are going to use children's oral language competencies and help them to take further steps in their reading development.

> While the child is trying to work out what reading is, and how he should work at it, natural language texts draw on his oral language competencies and allow him to build bridges across to more literary texts. (Clay 1991, p. 191)

If we revisit the 'to–with–by' continuum and the different strands or components of a comprehensive literacy program, language experience would stretch right across the continuum (see figure 2.1). A language-experience approach will usually include:

- modelled, shared or interactive writing to compose the text
- reading aloud and shared reading of the text
- independent reading of the text

A language-experience approach can also include:

- use of the text for guided writing
- independent writing about the shared experience

For reasons already noted, the language-experience strand is a very important component of your comprehensive literacy program. However, it has particular success with struggling readers, older non-readers, and with people who do not have English as their first language. (Meek 1983; Rigg 1989, 1990). Paulo Freire also had incredible success helping illiterate adults in South American countries. As a starting point, he would use shared experiences such as working in the fields. He helped many illiterate adults to become literate through a language-experience approach based on their daily activities.

Reading: different texts for different purposes

A wide range of texts

You will use a wide range and variety of books and other forms of text in your classroom.

Literature will be at the heart of your reading program. Literature has qualities and values which are not found in other reading materials, or in any other area of the curriculum. You will also use high-quality non-fiction books. You will need texts of all kinds and for many different purposes. As well as the children's books already mentioned (which are available to the whole community in good local book stores) you will also use materials produced by educational publishers specifically for school reading programs. The one rule is that the books used from 'school reading programs' must still have authentic text. They must have been written for an authentic purpose: to entertain, to inform, to explain, to tell a story, to describe, to persuade, and so on. If the authentic purpose has not been degraded by the instructional purpose, then you are much more likely to have a quality text. Beware of the books that have been written for instructional purposes only, and which have unnatural language: 'Nan can fan Dan' is out!

It's worth noting here that most children *can* learn to read from texts such as 'Nan can fan Dan' because they have brains which are capable of incredibly powerful learning. So their brains may learn to read 'Nan can fan Dan', but their hearts are untouched. What do they learn *about* reading from such inane nonsense? They learn things we don't want them to learn; they learn attitudes that turn them off reading. So, they learn to read, but they may choose never to do so.

> We are teaching human beings with feelings, values and emotions; we are not teaching robots. If we want children to become readers for life, we must say something to their hearts as well as their intellects.

The importance of literature

One of the most powerful ways of helping children become readers for life is to give them a love of literature. And the most powerful way of giving them a love of literature is to let them hear it read with passion. Viewing good quality videotapes or films can also be very effective. Many 'reluctant' readers have discovered literature through film. We have seen reluctant readers tackle books because they have seen and enjoyed the video first.

If the reading habit is not caught in the primary, or elementary, school, it may never be caught at all. The research over many years, and our experience, overwhelmingly supports the belief that literature will do more to motivate reading than any other single factor. Literature must be the heart of the reading program. There are many references supporting the use of literature as an ***essential*** ingredient in the classroom reading program. To start with, you may like to review some of the following:

Butler, Dorothy 1980, *Babies Need Books,* London: Bodley Head.

Chambers, Aidan 1985, *Booktalk,* London: Bodley Head.

Chomsky, Carol 1972, 'Stages in language development and reading exposure,' *Harvard Educational Review,* 42, February, 1–33.

Daniels, Harvey 1994, *Literature Circles: Voice and Choice in the Student-centered Classroom.* York, Maine: Stenhouse Publishers

Fader, Daniel 1976, *The New Hooked On Books,* New York: Berkley Publishing Corporation.

Harwayne, Shelley 1992, *Lasting Impressions: Weaving Literature into the Writing Workshop.* Portsmouth NH: Heinemann.

Hickman, J. & Cullinan, B. (eds) 1989, *Children's Literature in the Classroom: Weaving Charlotte's Web,* Norwood MA: Christopher Gordon.

Hornsby, D., Sukarna, D. & Parry, J. 1986, *Read On: A Conference Approach to Reading,* Sydney: Horwitz Martin. (Also Portsmouth NH: Heinemann, 1988)

Hornsby, D., Ferry, M. & Luxford, M. 1989, *Novel Approaches: Using Literature in the Classroom,* Melbourne: Nelson ITP.

Huck, C. 1989, 'No wider than the heart is wide', in *Children's Literature in the Classroom: Weaving Charlotte's Web,* eds J. Jickman & B. Cullinan, Norwood MA: Christopher-Gordon, pp. 251–62.

Huck,, C., Hepler, S., & Hickman, J. 1993, *Children's Literature in the Elementary School,* 5th edn, San Diego: Harcourt Brace Jovanovich.

Meek, Margaret 1983, *Achieving Literacy,* London: Routledge & Kegan Paul.

Moffett, James 1987, *Active Voices II,* Portsmouth NH: Heinemann.

Saxby, M. & Winch, G. 1987, *Give Them Wings: The Experience of Children's Literature,* Melbourne: Macmillan.

Veatch, J. 1968, *How to Teach Reading with Children's Books,* Katonah NY: Richard C. Owen.

Texts for reading aloud

As a guiding principle, books for ***reading to*** children will usually be books they can not yet read for themselves. They will be books that are rich in meaning, and books that extend the children's range of language features and structures. They will often be books from the school library (especially picture-story books, short stories, poems and novels, but also a range of non-fiction texts). It is important for children to hear text that they cannot yet read for themselves, because:

- they focus on meaning and have more opportunity to 'sink into' the book
- they form mental images related to the characters and the developing storyline
- they hear new and interesting language structures and features
- they are free to attend to aspects of text such as mood and style
- they hear new vocabulary in a context that helps them to build word meanings
- they learn more about how written texts work
- they are introduced to new authors
- they hear 'how reading works' and are motivated to do it themselves

If children can read a particular text on their own, we should ask, *Why aren't they?* However, when you have an educational purpose, you will sometimes read materials that many of the children would be capable of reading themselves. Some of these purposes might be:

- to introduce or revisit an author, illustrator, or author/illustrator
- to introduce 'series' and sequels

- to show your love for a particular text
- to broaden knowledge of the range of texts available
- to show that 'good, easy books are also allowed and honoured in that classroom' (Allington & Cunningham 1996, p. 46)

You will want to read one of your personal favourites, even if the children are capable of reading it themselves. For example, if you love *The Day the Wind Changed* by Ruth Park, and you laugh at the humour of it every time, you will want to share that humour with the children and show them that you love reading too.

You may wish to read a 'sure fire winner' such as *Rohan of Rin* (Emily Rodda) with the expectation that many children will then read the sequel, *Or Tales of a Fourth Grade Nothing* (Judy Blume) in the hope that some children will then read *Superfudge*.

You may read a *Bangers and Mash* book to introduce the characters to the children, and then show them other books from the series. A quick discussion of some of the titles and front cover illustrations will help the children when they are choosing their own book.

Texts for shared reading

For shared reading, you will use a huge variety of books and other printed materials. Big books, specifically designed for shared reading, usually provide text that all children can see easily. They are usually favourite titles, and will be used regularly over several days. They may be revisited at later times of the year as well.

However, you can do shared reading as long as all children in the class or the group can see a copy of the text. Sometimes, you might do shared reading from text being projected from an overhead transparency. At other times, you might have multiple copies of one book that you use for shared reading. Occasionally, in the middle and upper grades especially, you will find a newspaper article that is appropriate, and you can make multiple copies to use it for shared reading. Sometimes, copies of a pamphlet could be used. Very successful shared reading lessons have been taken with pamphlets about topics such as the European wasp, immunisation, rubbish collection and music festivals. Some selections from published reading scheme anthologies are often appropriate for shared reading as well.

It is important that the texts you use for shared reading are texts that the children want to return to. You might introduce the text on Monday, but each other day of the week you will revisit the text for further reading and related activities. As always, the text should be rich in meaning and the content should reflect the interests of the children.

Texts for guided reading

High quality

The books used for guided reading should have the same high quality as the books you use for any other purpose. They should be books that the children want to return to after the first reading.

Sets of books published specifically to support school reading programs have improved dramatically in recent years. Good publishers have kept up to date with developments in the theory and practice of reading and in their knowledge of the best conditions for helping children to read. They have been more concerned about

- meaning and text quality
- plot, character, setting, mood, style in fiction titles
- appropriate content (and how it is organised) in non-fiction titles
- attractive presentation and sensible layout
- suitable print size and word spacing
- balance of supports and challenges to help children make sense of text
- provision of books that provide increasingly more difficult challenges so that teachers are able to match children and texts as children make progress
- provision of books that allow children to practise over and over the skills and strategies they have learned
- a balance of text types and forms

In all published series there will be some disappointing titles that 'let us down'. These titles are more commonly found in the books published for beginning and emergent readers, as these levels are very difficult to write for. But at all levels, choose fiction titles (or selections in anthologies) that have literary merit, or that have a legitimate purpose. Choose non-fiction texts that present information clearly, logically and at a level appropriate to the children who will be reading them. Choose texts that provide opportunities not just for 'learning to read' but also for 'reading to learn'.

Some of the simplest books published specifically for schools will be easy caption books or 'list' books. For example, a book about a zoo might be a simple list of the animals you might see there (on each page you will have a picture of one animal and a printed caption under it). A list is an authentic form of text and can be an appropriate starting point for guided reading at the emergent stage, especially when the children have intrinsic interest in the topic. These simple caption books are certainly nothing like the 'Nan can fan Dan' variety.

Matching books to children's needs

You need to select books that match the children's needs. Ongoing observation and assessments, such as running records or records of reading behaviours, will give you the information you need about the children. Selection from an appropriately graded set of books will then be a relatively simple matter. (This aspect is discussed in more detail in chapter 3.)

Unseen texts

During guided reading, we want the children to use and practise strategies they *already* know to tackle text they do *not* know. Therefore, we need to keep a supply of unseen texts specifically for guided reading. After using a title in a guided reading session, you put it in that group's borrowing box to reread during silent reading time or at other opportunities. (Many schools choose not to send these books home, because the children often have younger brothers and sisters who will be starting school in a few years. If they have heard the books read at home, those books will no longer be unfamiliar and will therefore be less appropriate for guided reading.)

One of the most important reading strategies is the ability to make predictions as you read the text. If a familiar book is used, there is little left to predict. It is only with unfamiliar or unseen texts that children have opportunities to practise their predictions skills, along with all the other reading skills and strategies, to construct meaning for that text.

The need for multiple copies

Multiple copies are essential for effective group teaching. Each child in the group must have his or her own copy of the book. (Sharing one book between two children may be a temporary necessity, but only until the school can provide extra copies.)

The need for short texts that can be read in one session

In each guided reading session, we want children to use all the reading strategies involved in reading a selection from beginning to end: we want them to use strategies for predicting, for confirming or modifying predictions, for rejecting predictions and self-correcting if necessary. We want them to find out, in the context of the whole story, if their predictions were accurate or reasonable. We want to interact with them as they respond to the text while reading it from beginning to end. We want to see how they gradually reconstruct the author's intended meaning. We want them to reflect on the piece, and to discuss and compare what they thought with what actually happened. These, and other important reading behaviours, are best practised when a complete text is read in one session.

For children in the emergent, early and transitional (fluent) stages, it is preferable to experience all the important reading behaviours with a complete text, and in the one session. Therefore it is essential to have texts which are short enough to be read in one session.

For children who are self-extending and advanced readers, it is still important to provide short texts that can be read in one session, but the use of longer texts will now sometimes be appropriate. If you need short texts that can be read in one session by children in these stages, the short stories found in children's magazines and 'reading scheme' anthologies can be ideal. When you use longer texts, such as the very short junior novels currently being published, it might be necessary to extend the guided reading over two sessions. The 'mini-novels' have short chapters (maybe only five or six pages) but there are only a few lines of text on each page, and plenty of illustrations. You might use them over two sessions, or you might use a guided reading session to 'get the children into the book' and then let them finish reading independently. However, it is important for all children at all levels to experience the complete reading of a text in one session, so you will need to build up the supply of short stories and other suitable texts for use at the self-extending and advanced stages. 'Mini-novels' may sometimes be used over two sessions, but that should not become your standard practice.

'Real' books and 'reading scheme' books

'Real' books (published for the general market) and 'reading scheme books' are not necessarily opposites. Many books published specifically for school reading programs are outstanding books. It's also true that many 'real' books are trash. Each book must be judged on its own merits. Whether the book is a 'real' book or a 'reading scheme' book is not the issue, but there are some important things to consider.

There are thousands of general books that are useful for guided reading, and which could be available in multiple copies so that guided reading groups are possible. However, many teachers prefer to use these books for reading aloud and shared reading, since they can then focus more on appreciation and reader response. They believe that our best literature should be used as literature, and not for guided reading.

You will also be aware that the general books used in schools are available through local book stores, and often bought for children at home. For many children, they will be familiar books – and guided reading mostly requires unseen books.

Texts for independent reading

An effective and comprehensive literacy program requires that children have access to a very large supply of reading materials with a broad spread of easier and harder books. The materials will include the general books as well as the materials from reading programs published specifically for schools, and books published by the children themselves.

There will be a time every day that is devoted to silent independent reading. However, there will be many other times during the day when children may choose to read independently, so the classroom library and the main school library should both be accessible at all times.

You need to keep the materials from the 'reading schemes' aside until you require them for specific teaching purposes (especially shared and guided reading). However, after you have used a shared reading title, you can add it to the classroom library for the children to borrow at any time. After using a guided reading title, you should add it to that group's borrowing box, so that each child in the group can reread the book at their leisure. When the children in the group have had opportunities to reread a particular title, you can put that title back with the general supply of guided reading books.

School and classroom libraries

There will be a main school library with a substantial collection of materials, and a general classroom library in every room. The classroom library should be updated constantly by bringing books in from the main school library. The classroom library in particular makes books accessible to children, because the books are right in front of them. This has been shown to have positive effects on the amount of reading children do both inside the school and outside it (Fractor et al 1993).

There may also be computers, with on-line material to be read, or educational CD-ROM multimedia programs. Children might also be encouraged to bring books from their local library, or books from home.

Well-stocked school libraries, with teacher-librarians who are passionate about their role in the school, are essential. In some places, school libraries are in decline. Teacher-librarians are being replaced by part-time technicians who keep the books shelved, but don't have the background or enthusiasm that turns kids on to books. Tragically, some schools no longer have librarians or technicians, and libraries are becoming neglected. *A school without a fully functioning library is like a hospital without supplies. Nothing much will happen to prolong a reader's life.*

Schools have to take reading seriously. Yet an analysis of some school budgets shows that more money is spent on disposable worksheets and materials for 'busy work' than on books. To reach recommended targets in school and classroom libraries, most schools will need to spend more money, or allocate money in different ways. Allington and Cunningham (1996) suggest that classroom libraries in lower grades should have at least 700 books, and that classroom libraries in upper grades should have at least 400 books. How does your classroom measure up?

Schools today often have more flexibility over staffing than in previous years, so it would be sensible to think of having flexible hours for teacher-librarians. Children need to access libraries at lunch times and after school.

Reading: supports and challenges in text

When looking at the texts used for reading, we can reconsider the 'to–with–by' chart in light of the supports and challenges in text. If there are more challenges than supports, you will most likely need to read the book to the children. Alternatively, the book can be left until a more appropriate stage in the children's development. If there is a balance between the challenges and the supports in the text, then using the book for shared reading will be most appropriate. If there are plenty of supports, but several things which would challenge the children, then you will possibly choose to use that book for guided reading. If the text is easy, with plenty of supports to help the reader, then the book should be used for independent reading.

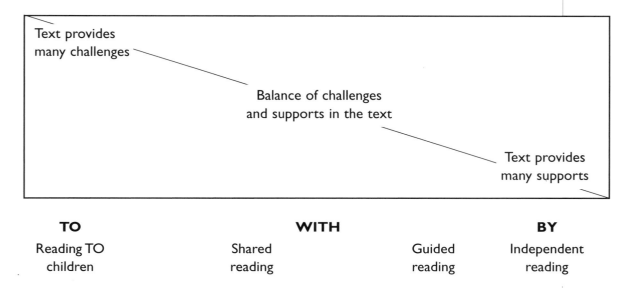

TO	**WITH**		**BY**
Reading TO children	Shared reading	Guided reading	Independent reading

Figure 2.6 Text supports and challenges

Component	Supports and challenges	Texts
Reading to children	The text is too difficult for children to read themselves.	An individual book for the teacher. (***not*** levelled)
Shared reading	The text has many challenges, but sufficient supports to enable children to enter into the reading with your support.	Big books Classroom charts with large print, including language-experience texts Multiple copies of a single title Text on overhead transparency Photocopied texts (eg newspaper articles) (***not*** levelled)
Guided reading	The text has enough supports to enable children to read most of the text independently. The challenges can be overcome when the teacher helps the children to apply known strategies.	Multiple copies of a single title Emergent, early and transitional (fluent) readers: text carefully matched to the group's needs. Reading Recovery levels help us to do this efficiently. Self-extending and advanced readers: wider range of criteria for book selection (content, theme, interest, form of text, conceptual load, vocabulary, etc) (levelled)
Independent reading	The text is easy, or familiar. It can be read with at least 95% accuracy. (Many researchers would say that children should be able to read the text with 97% accuracy or better.)	A wide variety and range of all kinds of texts, at all levels Lots of literature Lots of non-fiction Guided reading books available only to children who have already read the book with you, or to children reading at higher levels for guided reading (***not*** levelled)

Figure 2.7 Different materials for different purposes: a summary

Take-home reading

> The main aim of the 'take-home' reading program is that children will share positive reading experiences with other people who are significant in their lives.

We know that children have more positive attitudes to reading, and make better progress, when they are supported at home by parents or guardians who provide constructive and enjoyable literacy experiences. Nevertheless, some traditional practice (which has had more to do with 'historical accident' than careful thought) leads to tension and conflict at home. For example, some parents labour under the belief that their children should always be able to read the take-home book independently, or that their children must read everything orally, or that they should have a different book every night, and so on. Let's consider some of these issues by addressing some of the most common questions teachers and parents ask.

Do children choose their own take-home books?

Generally yes, but you also guide their choice, and sometimes even require them to take a particular book. You will monitor their choices and ensure that they are taking home books they can read independently, but you must also let them take home books they are keen to borrow, even if they are beyond their independent reading level.

But shouldn't children always be able to read their take-home book independently?

No. It is essential for children to take books they *can* read independently, as we want them to have lots of practice of easy reading, and we want them to celebrate their success with their families. However, they will sometimes choose books which are too difficult for independent reading. In this case, the parents will read the books *with* the children, or even *to* the children. Many schools now send a sheet home and ask the parents to tick or initial a 'to' column, a 'with' column, or a 'by' column. This written record is telling the teacher: 'I read the book *to* my child,' or 'I read the book *with* my child,' or 'My child read the book *by* him/herself.' The headings on top of a typical sheet are:

Date	Title	To child	With child	By child	Comments

The note on the bottom of the sheet was:

> Your child will bring home a wide selection of books. Please tick the 'to' column if you read the book to your child, the 'with' column if you read it together and helped your child, and the 'by' column if your child read the book independently. Please note that we expect to see equal numbers of ticks in each of the columns. Thankyou.

Don't we have to level the take-home books?

No. Children select from a wide range of reading materials. They take books from the school library, as well as books from the classroom library. However, you will monitor their borrowing to ensure that they take home books for independent reading, for sharing with parents, and for parents to read to them. In your supply of books for taking home, you will have books with known Reading Recovery levels, or books that have been levelled in some way for emergent, early, transitional, self-extending and advanced readers. As the teacher, you will know what the levels are, even though they won't be written on the books. You can ensure that, for independent reading, the children take home books that are on a lower level than those used for guided reading at school. For example, if children are reading books at school with a Reading Recovery level of 15 (with your guidance) then they should be taking home books that are level 11 or 12 or thereabouts. We want to ensure that they experience successful, independent reading.

Should children always be required to read aloud?

No. They will want to read aloud to demonstrate their successful reading, and parents will want to hear them read aloud too. However, a child may choose to read the entire book silently, and then just read a favourite page or two to parents. Or a child may read half the book quietly, and then read the last half to a parent, or older brother or sister.

Can we expect that all children will be supported at home?

Sadly, no. Most parents or guardians are very keen to help their children as much as possible, but there are all kinds of legitimate reasons why it is difficult for some children to get the support they need. Some parents are very busy and pressured by their own work demands, and then by the demands of looking after children and running a household. Others may speak and read in a language other than the language of instruction at school and be unable to help their children read the take-home book. However, if they understand the importance of home reading, they will provide the time and space required by the child to do the reading, and will discuss the book with their child. Discussion about the book would be legitimate, even in their own first language.

Sadly too, some parents may not understand the value of reading themselves, or they may have had negative life experiences which soured their attitudes towards education. Obviously, every school has to know its community and develop a take-home reading policy that reflects the reality of that community.

CHAPTER 3

Getting ready for guided reading

Knowing the children

Assessment as the starting point

Assessment is a continual process, not an event. Certainly, there will have been continual assessment of the children *before* you start guided reading with them. To form guided reading groups, you need to know which children in your class are beginning readers, emergent readers, early readers, and so on.

You need to know the children's strengths and needs for effective teaching/learning to occur. You need to know about their reading strategies, their reading behaviours, and their attitudes to reading. When you know this, you can group them appropriately, and select texts with the required supports and appropriate challenges. You can also provide the right level of teacher support so that they read the text independently. If you provide too much support, you take away opportunities to learn; if you provide too little support, you fail to provide the scaffolding necessary for independent reading. Assessment provides much of the information you need in order to determine the optimum amount of support.

Assessment through daily literacy events

Assessment starts by finding out what children know and what they *can do*, and only then concerns itself with discovering what they can't do. Daily, you gather evidence for what children can do. Very often, this will be done through the normal literacy activities in the classroom, because powerful teaching procedures also provide opportunities for effective assessment. Authentic assessment links teaching, learning and evaluation in important ways. If you have a knowledge of literacy development (and you know what to look for) then authentic assessment *informs* your teaching.

So, before you start guided reading with the children in your class, you will assess their reading strategies, behaviours and understandings through the normal literacy events that occur through the other strands of the program, such as shared reading, language-experience approach, and the components or strands of the writing program as well.

Johnston (1997, p. 2) reminds us that the word 'assessment' derives from the Latin word *assidere*, which means 'to sit alongside'. Johnston argues convincingly that assessment activities should 'help children become more reflective and engaged and more in control of their learning'. When you literally 'sit alongside' children as they are engaged in reading and writing, you gather the most telling and authentic assessment data. For the children, most of the assessment situations appear to be no different from familiar teaching/learning situations. For example, during the familiar shared reading procedure, you may be focusing carefully on several children, assessing their concepts about print, or their knowledge of letter names, or their ability to find specific spelling patterns. All this assessment can happen without the children even realising it.

Other assessment procedures

In addition to the assessments you make during familiar literacy activities, you will also be assessing the children through a range of more structured assessment procedures. But even these procedures can involve children in situations which feel 'comfortable' because they are very similar to those activities that are a common part of the daily classroom program, or they are procedures that are used often by the teacher and have become very familiar.

These more structured procedures will include running records, records of reading behaviours, word identification tests, letter identification tests, and so on. Certainly, Marie Clay's *Observation Survey* (1993) will help this kind of assessment and is widely used. The Primary Language Record (Barrs 1989) also provides very useful information. The assessment handbook edited by Lynn Rhodes (1993) has some particularly good instruments, especially for readers beyond the early stage. Since the more formal assessment procedures are described in detail in many excellent teacher references, they are not described here. However, the reference section at the end of book gives you details of some of the most readily available references.

Every child is ready to learn more!

Starting with what the children know, you can tailor your guided reading lessons to suit their strengths, needs and interests. Your knowledge of the children and the flexibility of your program mean that every child is ready to learn more. They are always ready when they are involved in a program that requires their involvement and provides the necessary support for their participation. (Indeed, it is the right of every child to receive the support they need for participation at their level.)

Grouping the children

Ability groups or mixed groups?

For guided reading, we work with groups of children who are similar in reading ability and working within the same developmental stage. The groups are flexible and based on constant and systematic observation and assessment. Ability groups are *essential* for guided reading at the emergent, early and transitional (fluent) stages, but sometimes, with children in the later developmental stages (self-extending and advanced) it can be appropriate to group in ways that allow them to read about a common interest or topic.

For all other strands of your reading program, you will use mixed-ability groups. Obviously, when you read to the whole class, you are reading to a mixed-ability group. In a language-experience cycle, you also use mixed-ability groups, and in shared reading, groups usually *should* be mixed ability. All children benefit from working with other children at different developmental stages every day. The following examples help to explain the benefits of mixed-ability groups.

When Debbie Sukarna was teaching at Mill Park Primary School, she had one boy, Phillip, who came into her year 5 class with records indicating that he was only reading at the 'early' stage. Observation and assessment during the first few weeks of school confirmed it. However, Phillip had also shown his passion for everything to do with planes and flying. He used to drive his parents crazy, asking them to take him to Melbourne Airport every weekend. If you were in the school ground, and a plane flew overhead, Phillip would come running to tell you what kind of plane it was, when it was made, how many passengers it would seat, how far it could fly, how long the pilots had to train to fly it, and a thousand other things. Debbie saw the opportunity of using the big book *At The Airport* for shared reading with a mixed-ability group including Phillip.

Debbie's purpose for the other children, who were independent readers, was obviously to have them read for meaning, but also to focus on information reports as a genre, and the structure of that text type. Her main purpose for Phillip was to put him in a 'win-win' situation where he would be able to draw on his considerable experience and contribute semantic information to the group, but also benefit from the ability of the other children who would be able to read most of the individual words in the text with little difficulty. Indeed, Phillip became the 'expert' in the group. He took meaning *to* the text and helped the others to get meaning *from* it. But Phillip also needed the others, most of whom had little difficulty with the text itself. Shared reading provides a 'win-win' situation with all members of the group working cooperatively to make meaning for the text.

Cooperative, mixed-ability groups have been found to increase achievement (Slavin 1983) so mixed-ability groups are common. But flexible, needs-based ability groups for focused teaching/learning are effective as long as they are constantly reviewed in the light of observation and assessment. Needs-based groups are certainly appropriate for guided reading but it is important for us to remember the warnings about fixed, inflexible ability groups:

- Streaming, tracking, and similar methods for assigning children on the basis of ability does not enhance achievement, and children in low groups rarely move to a higher group.
- Children's concepts of themselves as learners suffer when they are placed in 'the low group', and learning is impaired.
- Typically, children in low groups have received instruction which actually reduced the amount of time they spent reading.

You can read more about these concerns in Allington 1994; Allington & McGill-Franzen 1989; Filby et al 1982; Good & Marshall 1984; Hiebert 1983; and Hiebert & Taylor 1994.

How many groups?

Many teachers find that they can manage four groups, and that four groups are usually necessary to cover the range of reading abilities in the class, or to make the groups small enough. If you have four groups, you can run up to two groups 'back to back' each day. To fit the guided reading groups into the time allowed each day, you can see one of the groups that takes less time and then one of the groups that takes more time. In the middle and upper grades, many (if not all) of the children will be self-extending or advanced readers, but you will probably still need to have four groups so that group size is small enough for effective interaction. Even if all your children are advanced readers (reading beyond the Reading Recovery levels) they will still have different needs and have reached different levels of reading maturity, so grouping will still be required. The examples on pages 57–64 will help you think about the possibilities.

Optimum group size

We know that small group work is effective for many reasons. One is that children actually teach each other and learn from each other. All children in the group hear the comments, the questions and the discussion of others in the group, and all have a chance to contribute.

Small group teaching can be more effective than one-on-one teaching. But what is the optimum group size for guided reading? Pinnell & Fountas (1998) suggest that groups range from 2 to 8 children. Iversen & Reeder (1998) believe that the optimum group size is 6. For the purposes of discussion, let's suggest that the optimum size of a guided reading group is 5–6 children, but that 8 children would be the largest workable group.

Obviously, there are several factors which you will consider when forming guided reading groups. We have to consider our assessment data and the children's needs, but we also have to consider management issues. How many groups can we manage in the time we have?

Three groups rarely result in groups that are small enough. Currently, in Californian schools (where classes are not allowed to exceed 20 children) it may be possible to organise three groups of 6 or 7 children, but that assumes the children will fall neatly into three needs-based groups of roughly equal size. Obviously, you could not manage one emergent group of 4 children, one early group of 3 children, and then one huge transitional (fluent) group of 13 children. So even in classes of 20, you may need to form four groups.

One of the major concerns in schools is class size. In classes of more than 24 or 25 children, we often have to make compromises. If the range of abilities and needs is wide, six or seven groups may seem necessary, but it would be impossible to manage them in the time available, or it would mean that you work with each group less frequently.

If your class size is making it difficult to form groups of optimum size at every developmental stage, you will need to give priority to making the earlier groups smaller than the more advanced groups. For children not making the progress we would like to see, a group of 3 or 4 might be optimum. However, for a group of children beyond the stage we might expect, a larger group can work.

Typically, four groups will allow for your needs and the children's needs to be met. Sometimes, five groups may be necessary. The following examples will help you to think about the possibilities.

Grouping possibilities

Sample 1: First year at school (prep, kinder, or reception)

Mon	Tues	Wed	Thur	Fri
Group 1 Extra LEA & SR	Group 1 Extra LEA & SR	Group 2	Group 3	Group 3
Group 2	Group 3	Group 4	Group 2	Group 4

LEA = language-experience approach
SR = shared reading

Group 1 – Beginning Stage   Guided Reading not appropriate. Will do extra shared reading and language-experience to help them work towards the emergent stage and prepare for guided reading.

Group 2 – Emergent   (RR levels 1–2)   3 days/week
Group 3 – Emergent   (RR levels 3–5)   3 days/week
Group 4 – Early   (RR levels 6–8)   2 days/week

Sample 2: Year 1A (four different groups at three different developmental stages)

Mon	Tues	Wed	Thur	Fri
Group 1	Group 1	Group 2	Group 3	Group 1
Group 2	Group 3	Group 4	Group 2	Group 3

Group 1 – Emergent   (RR levels 3–5)   3 days/week
Group 2 – Early   (RR levels 6–8)   3 days/week
Group 3 – Early   (RR levels 9–11)   3 days/week
Group 4 – Transitional (RR levels 12–14)   1 day/week

If you have a greater number of children at any one developmental stage, you may need to have two groups as shown in this sample. Group 2 would be 'early' early readers (possibly reading books with Reading Recovery levels 6–8) and Group 3 would be 'late' early readers (possibly reading books with Reading Recovery levels 9–11).

Sample 3: Year 1B (four different groups at four different developmental stages)

If you had some experienced, self-extending readers in a year 1, they would not require an intensive guided reading session with you every day. You should try to take the group at the lowest developmental stage as often as possible, because you will be concerned to lift their reading ability.

Mon	Tues	Wed	Thur	Fri
Group 1	Group 1	Group 2	Group 1	Group 1
Group 2	Group 3	Group 4	Group 2	Group 3

Group 1 – Emergent   (4 days/week; about 10 minutes each day = 40 mins/week)

Group 2 – Early   (3 days/week; 12–15 minutes each day = about 40 mins/week)

Group 3 – Transitional   (2 days/week; 15–20 minutes each day = 30 to 40 mins/week)

Group 4 – Experienced   (1 day/week; 20–25 minutes/week)

One guided reading session a week for the experienced (self-extending) readers is more than sufficient, as these children will be doing a lot more reading in the literature strand and other strands of the program. If they become experienced readers during year 1, then they are doing very well.

Sometimes, for Group 1, or for any other groups who experience difficulty with a particular text, you could consider using one text on two different days. For example, you could use one text for guided reading on Monday, and revisit it on Tuesday for more independent reading. If you use the same text a second time, you will expect a different level of achievement from the children, and a greater emphasis on reader response.

Sample 4: Year 2 (five groups)

Mon	Tues	Wed	Thur	Fri
Group 1	Group 1	Group 2	Group 1	Group 1
Group 2	Group 2	Group 3	Group 4	Group 4
Group 3	Group 3	Group 5 perhaps alternate weeks only		

Group 1 – Early	(RR levels 9–11)	(4 days/week)
Group 2 – Transitional (fluent)	(RR levels 12–14)	(3 days/week)
Group 3 – Transitional (fluent)	(RR levels 15–17)	(3 days/week)
Group 4 – Self-extending	(RR levels 18–22)	(2 days/week)
Group 5 – Advanced	(beyond RR levels)	(1 day each second week)

With five groups, it is probably necessary to plan for three guided reading lessons on two or three days of the week.

Group 1 might be only a small group of three children in the early developmental stage, but if they are still at the early stage in year 2, you will want them to participate in guided reading sessions at least four days each week.

There are more children in the transitional (fluent) stage than the other stages, and too many for one group. So they are split into groups 2 and 3. The Group 2 children are reading within Reading Recovery levels 12–14, and the Group 3 children are reading within Reading Recovery levels 15–17. For these children, three guided reading sessions per week are planned.

If children have reached the advanced reading stage during year 2, they are making excellent progress, and you might decide that a guided reading session once every second week is sufficient. One session each week would be possible but advanced readers should be spending more time reading literature, reading for research, and so on.

Sample 5: Year 3

Mon	Tues	Wed	Thur	Fri
Group 1	Group 1	Group 2	Group 1	Group 1
Group 2	Group 3	Group 4	Group 2	Group 3

Group 1 – Early   (RR levels 9–11)   (4 days/week)
Group 2 – Transitional (fluent)   (3 days/week)
Group 3 – Self-extending (experienced)   (2 days/week)
Group 4 – Advanced   (1 day/week)

We would hope that all children in year 3 are beyond the early reading stage, but that is not always the case. Even if you have only two or three children at the early stage in year 3, it would be important to group them for guided reading. In addition, since they are still early readers, it would be preferable for them to meet with you for guided reading at least four days a week. Ten minutes on each of those four days will be more effective than 20 minutes on each of two days. The children will also benefit from the small group interactions.

When using texts that are suitable for early readers, it is possible to complete a guided reading session in 10 to 12 minutes. You may find that you have 15 minutes available, but 10 to 12 minutes will usually suffice. Compare the Group 1 time with the time you might spend with the other groups:

Group 1 Early readers: 4 x 12 minutes = 48 minutes per week
Group 2 Transitional readers: 3 x 15 minutes = 45 minutes per week
Group 3 Self-extending
         readers: 2 x 20 minutes = 40 minutes per week
Group 4 Advanced readers: 1 x 20 minutes = 20 minutes per week

Again, the advanced readers don't need the same amount of time on guided reading as the other groups. They are, after all, mature readers. They will be spending more of their time reading in the literature strand of the program, researching, 'reading to learn', and so on.

Sample 6: Year 4

Mon	Tues	Wed	Thur	Fri
Group 1	Group 1	Group 2	Group 4	Group 1
Group 2	Group 2	Group 3	Group 3	Group 4

Group 1 – Transitional   (3 days/week)
Group 2 – Self-extending   (3 days/week)
Group 3 – Advanced   (2 days/week)
Group 4 – Advanced   (2 days/week)

Note: You may need a group of just one or two children, especially if they are well below the level you would expect. For example, you may have just two children at the transitional stage, and you will bring them together as Group 1.

Sample 7: Year 3/4

The groups in a year 3/4 might fall out the following way:

Mon	Tues	Wed	Thur	Fri
Group 1	Group 1	Group 4	Group 1	Group 1
Group 2	Group 2	–	Group 3	Group 3

Group 1 – Transitional (fluent)   4 days/week
Group 2 – Self-extending (experienced)   2 days/week
Group 3 – Self-extending (experienced)   2 days/week
Group 4 – Advanced   1 day/week

Again, Group 1 will have more of your time over the week. However, if Group 4 is the only group you have on Wednesday, you can run a longer session for the children in that group.

Sample 8: Year 4

A year 4 might be grouped in the following way:

Mon	Tues	Wed	Thur	Fri
Group 1	Group 1	Group 3	Group 1	Group 1
Group 2	Group 2	Group 4	Group 2	Group 2

Group 1 – Transitional (fluent)   4 days/week
Group 2 – Self-extending (experienced)   4 days/week
Group 3 – Advanced   1 day/week
Group 4 – Advanced   1 day/week

In this classroom, there may be only two or three transitional readers, but since they are in year 4, it would be essential to meet with them for guided reading at least three or four times a week. They must be given every opportunity to develop their reading strategies and 'make up lost ground'. One guided reading session per week for the advanced readers is more than sufficient; they will be spending more time reading literature and working within the other strands of the program.

Sample 9: Year 5/6 A

Although at year 5/6 level we would hope that all children are advanced readers, some are still reading at the transitional stage, or have just reached the experienced (self-extending) stage. They need to have guided reading at least four days a week to give them the best chance of making the necessary progress into the advanced stage. Hopefully, you will have only one group of children who need guided reading four days a week in year 5/6.

How you group the other advanced readers in the class will depend upon class size as well as any differences in ability. Generally, you don't want a guided reading group of more than eight children (fewer if possible). However, groups may be slightly bigger than eight children if they are advanced, independent readers. In a large class (say 30) you might find that you have:

Group 1 – Self-extending
            (experienced)   3 children   4 days/week
Group 2 – Advanced   10 children   1 day/week
Group 3 – Advanced   10 children   1 day/week
Group 4 – Advanced   7 children   1 day/week

Mon	Tues	Wed	Thur	Fri
Group 1	Group 1	–	Group 1	Group 1
–	Group 2	Group 3	Group 4	–

The three Group 1 children would still be reading texts from Reading Recovery levels 18 to 20+. The other 27 children would be reading texts beyond the Reading Recovery levels. Sample criteria for providing appropriate texts beyond the Reading Recovery levels are listed on page 66.

The children in Groups 2, 3 and 4 are advanced or independent readers; they don't need guided reading more than once a week. They will still be involved in shared reading and language-experience, but most of the time they will be involved in the literature program and in reading to learn (reading for research).

With this arrangement, you would have only one guided reading group on Mondays, Wednesdays and Fridays, and two groups on Tuesdays and Thursdays.

Sample 10: Year 5/6 B

In another year 5/6, all the children may be reading texts beyond the Reading Recovery levels. They are all advanced readers, and one session of guided reading each week for each group is adequate. Most of the time, they are involved in a literature program, and reading as part of their research across all areas of the curriculum. They are also taking part in shared reading sessions, and are still being read to every day.

In a large class, you might form four guided reading groups of up to seven or eight children.

Mon	Tues	Wed	Thur	Fri
Group 1	Group 2	Group 3	Group 4	–

In a class of reasonable size, you may be able to run three groups of seven or eight children for guided reading, and devote more time to the other important strands of your reading program.

Mon	Tues	Wed	Thur	Fri
Group 1	–	Group 2	–	Group 3

Organisation of texts for guided reading

Levels of difficulty

Because it is essential to match books to the children for guided reading, it is necessary to use books that have been levelled according to known criteria. Different ways of levelling books are used in different countries, but the levels are always on a continuum, and the levels assigned to individual books may vary over time as trialling continues with children. Levels can only be suggested, but they do help you to select books for particular groups of children. When you are using the books with the children, you will be able to fine tune your own understanding of the levels and you will have more information about their suitability for guided reading for certain children.

Books used for other strands of your reading program are not levelled, and don't need to be.

You may be teaching for an employer who provides criteria for levelling. You may be teaching in a school district that has adopted broad bands based on Reading Recovery levels (see below). Fountas & Pinnell (1996) provide their own set of criteria for creating a text gradient. Their text gradient is not related to Reading Recovery levels, so teachers probably need to spend a lot of time applying the criteria and levelling. Whichever gradient or continuum you use, you need to know how it was established and how to apply it.

Collapsing Reading Recovery levels into broader groups

Using Reading Recovery levels as a basis for grouping and levelling books makes sense, because the Reading Recovery levels have become common in most English-speaking countries. Also, the Reading Recovery levels have become very reliable, because they have been trialled over time with many children. For these reasons, many education authorities (departments, states, districts, etc) have decided to use a continuum of text levels based on Reading Recovery levels.

However, the finely tuned but narrow Reading Recovery levels were designed specifically for children who need the extra assistance provided by small increases in the number of challenges in text. For children making normal progress or better, we can collapse the Reading Recovery levels into broader groups, or bands. Figure 3.1 shows how this has been done in New Zealand, Victoria (Australia) and England.

| Stage of development | New Zealand and Victoria (Australia) | | England | | |
	Groups	Reading Recovery levels	Bands	National Curriculum level	RR levels
Emergent	A	1–2	1	Working *towards*	1–2
	B	3–5	2	Level 1	3–5
Early	C	6–8	3	Working *within*	6–8
	D	9–11	4	Level 1	9–11
Transitional (fluent)	E	12–14	5	Working *within*	12–14
	F	15–17	6	Working *towards*	15–16
			7	Level 2	17–18
Self-extending (experienced)		18 +	SAT Level 2C	Working *within*	19–20
			SAT Level 2B	Level 2	21–22
			SAT Level 2A	Working *towards* Level 3	23–24

Figure 3.1 Reading Recovery levels and related groups or bands

In England, the Reading Recovery levels have been related to 'bands' at the emergent, early and transitional stages, and then to SAT levels at the self-extending and advanced stages (see page 19).

In New Zealand and Victoria (Australia) the Reading Recovery levels up to levels 17 or 18 are collapsed into groups and relate to the emergent, early and transitional (fluent) stages. When children have moved through the transitional stage and have started working within the self-extending stage, other criteria are often used to group books. However, some teachers may choose to continue using Reading Recovery levels as shown in figure 3.2.

Developmental stage	Reading Recovery levels	Levels > Groups	It can be useful to say ...
Emergent	1–5 or 6	1–2 Group A 3–5 Group B	Emergent A Emergent B
Early	6–11 or 12	6–8 Group C 9–11 Group D	Early C Early D
Transitional (fluent)	12–17 or 18	12–14 Group E 15–17 Group F	Transitional E Transitional F
Self-extending (experienced)	18 +	18 +	Self-extending
Advanced	Beyond Reading Recovery levels	n/a	Advanced
OR			
Self-extending (experienced)	18–23+	18–20 Group G 21–23 Group H	Self-extending G Self-extending H
Advanced	Beyond Reading Recovery levels	n/a	Advanced

Figure 3.2 Text groupings from Reading Recovery levels

Benchmark books

As you work with the books in each level (band or group) you will become very familiar with them. Any book that *consistently* provides the right balance of supports and challenges for children at the appropriate developmental stage could be kept aside and used as a benchmark book for that stage. Benchmark books are particularly useful for the ongoing assessment that is essential for providing the information you need for effective program planning.

'Easy' and 'hard' books

It is impossible to say that a book is 'easy' or 'hard'. To start with, the words are relative. We might ask: Easy or hard compared to what? Easy or hard for whom? Whether a book is easy or hard for a child will also depend on the support you are providing. So the books used for guided reading are placed on a **continuum** from easiest to hardest according to a wide range of characteristics, including subject matter, storyline, conceptual load, text complexity, sentence length, syntactic patterns, vocabulary, density of information, amount of print per page, size and type of print, use of illustrations, and so on. You will select books from this continuum to match the interests, strengths and needs of the children, as discussed in the next section.

Texts that are too difficult

A common finding is that children are often given guided reading and independent reading texts that are too difficult. For independent reading, we commonly use books that children can read with at least 95% word accuracy. However, for independent reading, many researchers would recommend that children should be given books they can read with 97–100% accuracy (ie no more than 3 unknown words in every hundred). It surprises many teachers that text has to be that 'easy' for effective independent reading – and it certainly surprises most parents. There is an unfortunate belief that you must give children 'hard' books if you are going to help them improve. You might have to convince some colleagues and parents that lots of easy independent reading can do more to improve reading than constant struggles with texts that are too difficult. (We will be using challenging books in the classroom, but they will be used for reading aloud and for shared reading.)

For guided reading, Fountas and Pinnell (1996) say: 'If the reader, with an introduction and support, cannot read about 90% of the words accurately, the text is too difficult.' They immediately point out that 'the accuracy analysis here is *not* a test of the reader but a test of the teacher's selection and introduction of the text.' The use of percentage accuracy alone is fraught with danger, as discussed below.

Use of percentage accuracy

The percentage accuracy is used only as a rough rule of thumb to make a quick but crude decision about the text difficulty level for a particular child. It is essential to consider the quality of the miscues as well as the quantity of them.

Marie Clay (1993) provides an instructive example. Two different children read the same piece of text. Both had 85% word accuracy. From percentage accuracy alone, you would conclude (incorrectly) that the text was at 'frustration' level for both children. Indeed, when you analyse the miscues that Child A made, you see that meaning was destroyed in every instance. When you analyse the miscues that Child B made, you see that meaning was maintained in every instance. Clearly, the text would be too difficult for guided reading for Child A, but it may be a suitable text for Child B.

Since the most proficient readers often make miscues that maintain meaning, many researchers and practitioners recommend that miscues maintaining meaning should be disregarded when calculating the percentage accuracy. For example, Eggleton (1992) writes:

> In analysing errors, consider what the error rate would be if unimportant errors are disregarded. Errors which do not alter meaning at all may be the kind of errors that proficient readers make. Working out the error rate including these errors may give a distorted view of the child's competence. (p. 17)

Disregarded or not, they must be considered.

Making judgments on percentage accuracy alone is very dangerous!

In addition, when the ideas or concepts in a book are unfamiliar for children, reading that text could also be more difficult than word accuracy alone would indicate. You might need to determine the children's prior knowledge of the ideas. If they are unfamiliar ideas, you will need to attend to the ideas during the book introduction, or use the book for shared reading rather than guided reading. Obviously, it is essential for you to *know* the book before you know how to use it for teaching purposes.

Matching children and texts

Getting started

1. As a result of your observations and assessment, you will know about the children's interests and the kinds of books they can manage with and without your help. If you have results for retellings and running records on books with known Reading Recovery levels, you will have information about the range of levels which is most likely to result in a child reading with 90–95% accuracy and with attention to meaning. Analysis of the miscues, and the retelling results, will help you determine whether individual children are reading for meaning or not.
2. Use this information to work out the first tentative groupings (see pages 54–64).
3. For one group at a time, browse the books you have for guided reading. If they are books that already have a Reading Recovery level, you will know which group of books to consider first. Scan the books for

features that will support the children, and for features that may be a challenge. If you believe the children in the group will be able to overcome the challenges with your help, you will consider the book for guided reading.

4. With your knowledge of the children and relevant assessment information, your selection will often match the children's needs very well. However, don't be disappointed if the match is not as close as you would like it to be. This whole business of matching books to children for guided reading is like trying on shoes: you start with an informed guess, but if one book doesn't 'fit', determine why, and then try another one.

5. If you are unsure, it is a good idea to start the children a level or two lower than you think is appropriate, so that they read with confidence. You can quickly move up to a level that you think is more appropriate. It's better for children to start with success on a slightly easier book than failure on a book that is too challenging.

Fine tuning

Once you start regular guided reading sessions with groups of children, you can use the guided reading session itself to collect further assessment data. As you observe the children, interact with them, and ask them questions, you will receive valuable information about how they are using the reading strategies, how they are comprehending the text, their level of involvement, and so on. In other words, guided reading is not just a teaching procedure; it is also a powerful assessment tool. Once you have made the initial match between the children and the texts, and continued with guided reading sessions, you will be able to 'fine tune' the match.

> Information gained during guided reading sessions will help you to 'fine tune' the future matches you make between the children and the books.

Starting guided reading with emergent readers

What to look for

In her book *Developing Life-Long Readers*, Margaret Mooney (1988, pp. 7–11) describes some attitudes, understandings, and behaviours that are characteristic of the emergent, early and transitional (fluent) stages. Mooney points out that they are not definitive or exhaustive, and that many of the characteristics in previous stages will continue to be evident in later stages. Leanna Traill, in *Highlight My Strengths: Assessment and Evaluation of Literacy Learning* (1993, pp. 25–7) describes attitudes, knowledge and skills at the emergent, early and fluency (transitional) stages as well.

These characteristics are like 'signposts'. A consideration of the emergent stage characteristics will help you to make the decision about when to start guided reading.

Many of the characteristics or 'signposts' will be evident as a result of your continuous observation and assessment. Once you know that some children are moving from the beginning stage into the emergent stage of reading, it will be time to consider grouping them for their first guided reading session.

Some questions to ask

Many resources will help you to formulate questions that will guide your decision-making. For example, Dorn, French & Jones (1998) suggest the following list of questions to help you decide when it might be appropriate to start guided reading groups for children. The list should not be used as a definitive checklist, but asking the questions will add to the information you already have.

- Do they have many of the early concepts of print almost under control (ie can they distinguish between text and illustration)?
- Do they have some understanding of directionality?
- Do they have some knowledge of one-to-one matching?
- Do they know the difference between letters and words?
- Do they know the letters of the alphabet?
- Do they know a few frequently encountered words (eg *I, the, a*)?
- Do they actively participate in shared reading by predicting events and language structures that show an awareness of comprehension, rhythm, and rhyme?
- Do they spend time reading and noticing a few details of print?
- Do they explore the print on the classroom's walls?
- Do they notice that the same words appear in many different contexts?
- Do they link sounds with symbols when they write?
- Do they articulate words slowly as they write?

You could also ask:

- Do they expect what they read to make sense?
- Do they return to favourite books?
- Do they think about what might happen in stories?
- Do they talk about the information in non-fiction books?

- Do they know some graphophonic relationships (especially for consonants)?
- Do they use picture cues and/or initial consonants to confirm predictions in shared reading?

If you can answer some of these questions with 'yes', and if your other assessment information supports the answers, then you will bring these children together and start guided reading with them.

Knowing the classroom program

What has already been taught

As the classroom teacher, you are involved with the children every day. You get to know them very well. You also know the overall language program you have been developing, and details of what your teaching program has been. This knowledge influences many of the decisions you make during guided reading sessions.

For example, if you are teaching children in their first year at school (prep, reception or kinder) and you know that you used the 'sound sense' fold-out called *Messy Mud*, then you know you helped all children consolidate or learn the relationship between the letter 'm' and a sound it commonly represents, /m/. Later, if an emergent group of readers is reading a zoo book, and they come across the word *monkey*, you know that you can challenge them with questions relating to the first letter of the word.

If you are teaching a group of transitional (fluent) readers in your year 2, and you know that you referred to the base word *aqua* (meaning water) in a science unit several weeks ago, then you know you can challenge children with that knowledge when they encounter a word such as *aquarium* in their guided reading text.

If you are using a non-fiction text for guided reading with a group of self-extending readers in your year 3/4, and you know that you helped them to use a glossary just two weeks ago, then you know you can question, prompt and challenge in ways that require the children to use their understanding of glossaries.

The classroom teacher is the best person to guide children's reading

In other words, knowing your classroom program helps you to challenge the children in ways that are not possible for other teachers. The classroom teacher who teaches all other aspects of the language program and the broader curriculum is in the best situation to provide appropriate supports and challenges for the children in guided reading groups. A strength of primary (elementary) classrooms is that the one teacher is responsible for most, if not all, of the curriculum and for all of the teaching/learning interactions that occur in the room.

> The *classroom teacher* is the best person to provide the appropriate supports and challenges for the children in guided reading groups. No other person has the same information about the children or the classroom program.

Learning expected behaviours in shared reading

Many of the common routines or behaviours that children will be using during guided reading can be taught and practised during the more relaxed, cooperative shared reading sessions. For example, when a text for shared reading has become familiar over two or three days, you could say to the children: *Read page x quietly with your eyes, and then look up at me. When everyone's ready, we'll talk about it.* When this has become an established practice, you can ask the children to do the same thing during guided reading and they will know what you expect.

You help the children become familiar with the ways in which we describe reading behaviours. You help them to become familiar with the instructions you give. You help them to know what you expect. Then, when you start guided reading with them, your instructions and requests are understood.

Because the children in a guided reading session are grouped by ability, they will have similar reading strengths and needs. They will usually have similar rates of reading as well. Even so, some children in the group may finish a short time ahead of others. Again, you can help them know what to do by explaining options during shared reading. The options could include rereading a favourite part, looking back through the illustrations, or checking unusual or difficult words encountered during the reading.

Teach the strategies in shared reading, apply them in guided reading

You demonstrate strategies in shared reading, over and over again. You talk about the strategies, and expect the children to 'take over this talk' for you. In other words, during shared reading, you help the children to learn and articulate the reading strategies. When you have done this, you can expect the children to use those strategies in guided reading.

Developing a supportive classroom climate

Classroom climate

It is important to develop a positive attitude to learning and a classroom climate in which children work together cooperatively. Children must know that it is 'safe' to express their ideas, to make predictions, to 'think aloud' in front of others. This is necessary for all learning; it is certainly no less important during guided reading sessions. We need to reinforce those things which develop the right climate for learning.

We must also work hard to develop a climate in which the group helps the individual. If a child contributes, but the contribution is incorrect or inappropriate, then the group helps to refine or correct the response.

No put-downs allowed

In reading, we know that the children who make the most rapid progress include those who are prepared to 'have a go'. Therefore, when children attempt the reading of any part of the text, or contribute to discussion, or express an opinion, they must know that their participation is going to be valued and their contribution received positively. If any child in the group demeans another, that child is politely but firmly asked to leave the group. If the established rule is 'No put-downs' then that child does not need a second chance. A second chance may simply give the message that a third chance might be given. Children learn that positive comments and cooperative behaviour are expected.

CHAPTER 4

A closer look at guided reading

Teacher preparation

Select an appropriate text

You have already assessed the children, observed their reading behaviours and set up groups for guided reading. For each group, you now select texts appropriate for guided reading. These will be texts that allow children to operate *within their zone of proximal development*: they will be texts that provide the supports children need to process the text using strategies they know, but they will also provide challenges which the children can overcome with your support.

If you are starting a group of children on guided reading for the first time, you might consider selecting a text which is easier for the children than your assessment would indicate. It is better for the children to have success rather than frustration when first experiencing a new teaching procedure. If you do happen to select a book that is a little too difficult, simply provide more support. In fact, your guided reading session may turn into a shared reading session. Nothing is lost. The children still benefit and you obtain more information to help you select more appropriately the next time.

It is sometimes claimed that you need to select a book that can be read at 90% accuracy or better. This is a 'rough rule of thumb' to make first decisions about book selection, but we must also remember to look at the quality of the miscues children make when they read. Percentage accuracy alone is not a sufficient indicator (see pages 67–8).

When the ideas or concepts in a book are unfamiliar for children, reading that text could also be more difficult than word accuracy alone would indicate. You might need to determine the children's prior knowledge of the ideas. If they are unfamiliar ideas, you will need to attend to the ideas during the book introduction, or use the book for shared reading rather than guided reading.

Obviously, it is essential to read the books to know whether they can be used for guided reading.

Determine a teaching focus

Determine a teaching purpose, or a focus, for the guided reading session. This will be based on your knowledge of what the children's needs are, what challenges they are ready to face, and what the book has to offer.

During the *emergent and early* stages, your teaching interventions focus on helping the children to make predictions, sample the text, confirm predictions, or modify predictions and make self-corrections if necessary. In other words, the focus is usually related to specific reading strategies, and may include:

- using text read so far to make predictions
- rereading
- searching for specific print information
- searching for information from illustrations
- using graphophonic knowledge to check predictions
- cross-checking

At the later developmental stages, the children are now coordinating and integrating the predicting, sampling, confirming and self-correcting strategies, and your teaching focus shifts to the meaning of larger sections of text, and the structure of the text. If the text is a retelling or a narrative, the more traditional aspects of character, setting, mood and style can also be a focus. If it is a non-fiction text, you might focus on information and the way it is presented.

The focus may be related to any of the following:

- a study skill such as locating an index entry and finding the relevant text in the book
- specialised vocabulary or concepts
- use of heading and subheadings
- text structure
- the author's writing style
- character
- literary devices such as alliteration, rhyme, metaphor, simile, exaggeration, personification

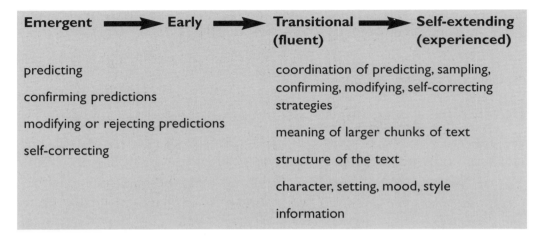

Figure 4.1 Possible teaching focuses

Plan independent work for the others

You will need to ensure that all other children are involved in independent work, or working with support staff or parent helpers. The question, 'What do I do with the others?' is discussed in chapter 6.

Format of a guided reading session

There are no recipes

There are no recipes or set procedures for guided reading. A major aim is to help children use reading strategies they already know in order to work out what they don't know, so that they read most of the text independently, with success. Obviously, there are different ways of achieving this.

For guided reading to be successful, you make many important decisions 'on the run'. This is not possible without sound professional knowledge. We are more likely to facilitate successful guided reading sessions when:

- we are teaching the other components of the literacy program in our classroom and we are capitalising on the essential links
- we know the children very well (their reading behaviours, understandings and attitudes)
- we know the texts being used for guided reading (including their supports and challenges)
- we understand the reading process (and know the reading strategies)
- we understand development in reading (and know the characteristics of the developmental stages)
- we use our common sense and trust our own judgment

Years ago, Donald Graves wrote that 'the enemy is orthodoxy'.

> …orthodoxies are substitutes for thinking. They clog our ears. We cease to listen to each other, clouding the issues with jargon in place of simple, direct prose about actual children. (1984 p. 185)

It would be a pity if arguments for 'one way' of doing guided reading led us to a set of orthodoxies which prescribed our practice and stood in the way of understanding. Sample lesson plans, like those in chapter 5, and those in many teacher's guides for published reading schemes, can provide some ideas and let you see how guided reading has sometimes worked with groups of children. However, there is no substitute for your own professional knowledge and the decisions you need to make.

There is no substitute for your own professional knowledge.

A consistent framework

The following four-part framework is a consistent feature in descriptions of guided reading:

Part 1:   Introducing the text
Part 2:   Reading the text
Part 3:   Revisiting the text
Part 4:   Responding to the text

Differences in practice exist mainly in part 2, and relate to how the independent reading of the text is guided (see pages 81 to 91). Two main approaches are described on the following pages. They are not 'opposing' or mutually exclusive approaches; they simply describe different levels of support for the learner. In fact, the art of teaching is knowing how much support to provide, and how much learner responsibility to expect. This is true in all teaching/learning situations, and is certainly true when helping children learn to read. The effective teacher will move backwards and forwards along the continuum between providing maximum support and expecting major learner responsibility. The effective teacher responds to how the children are managing the text, and 'changes gear' when necessary. You may start guiding a text very closely, but will 'change gear' if you see the children managing the challenges in the text independently. In other words, you may start with a 'very guided' approach, and move to a 'partly guided' approach.

Part 1: Introducing the text

Set the scene. Help children to formulate questions to keep in their minds while reading, and to make predictions about the text. Prepare the children to take control of the reading themselves.

Part 2: Reading the text

A: 'very' guided reading	B: partly guided reading	Components of A and B
Reading section-by-section (see pp. 83–85)	*Reading at own rate*	*Reading first few sections, then reading at own pace.*
Teacher guides the independent reading of the text section by section. Brief discussion between each section. Oral reading for real purposes. New predictions made before reading next section.	Children read the text orally, at own pace. Assistance from teacher when necessary. Activities required for early finishers.	Teacher starts guiding the reading section by section, but if the children indicate that they can manage the challenges in the text independently, the teacher encourages them to read on at their own pace.
Most useful when working with a group of children. Overcomes main problems associated with children in groups reading aloud.	Most useful when working with one child. If working with a group, individual children can hear others and 'parrot-read'.	Combines some of the best features of the alternatives described here.

Part 3: Revisiting the text

Reread the text, individually, in pairs, as a group – especially at the emergent and early stages (see pp 91–2).

Children ask their own questions, discuss content, express feelings and reactions.

Possible teaching points: linguistic features, vocabulary, text structure and layout, illustrations, author's style, etc.

Part 4: Responding to the text

Response is varied and personal. Response could be oral, artistic, dramatic, written.

Child may simply choose to read another book, which may be related by author, illustrator or topic. (Note: The best response to reading is to want to read more. The children are not required to do a set task or 'assignment' after every book.)

Place copies of the book in the group's borrowing box so that members of the group can choose the book to read again.

Introducing the text

The purpose of the book introduction

When introducing the text to the children, your main purpose is to 'set them up for success'. Your introduction will build adequate prior knowledge for the children to use, so that they have the best chance possible of reading the text independently. You 'tune them in' to the type of text, to the likely message of the text, and to features of the language. The introduction will be like a conversation, and must give the children access to the book.

You could give the children access to the **meaning** of the text by:
- giving a brief preamble about the story or the topic or the ideas in the book (for example: *This story is about something that happens to a pet dog* or *This book is about snakes*.
- discussing cover illustrations and perhaps one or two key illustrations inside the book
- discussing the title and any other relevant print information on the cover
- having the children discuss related experiences from their own lives (especially when the text is narrative or recount) and related knowledge (especially for non-fiction books)
- discussing the characters in the story
- reading a short way into the text.

You could give the children access to the **syntax**, or the structure of the language by:
- using some of that language in your introduction
- using the tense of the text in your discussion
- using language patterns found in the text
- 'casually' using any vocabulary which may be unfamiliar to the children
- asking questions in the same tense, number and gender as the text to which you are referring

If you think there are specific **words** or **spelling patterns** that are likely to be challenging, you could give children access to those words or graphophonic cues by:
- having them locate specific words
- introducing them to unfamiliar proper nouns
- having them notice any common spelling patterns
- having them identify letters, or letter clusters, in selected words
- having them look at the whole word' to see if it matches what they predicted

The degree of teacher involvement

Marie Clay (1991) writes about giving children access to unfamiliar story-books and helps us to worry less about telling the children too much about the story before they read it. Clay reminds us that in a conversation, the listener must know the speaker's prior experience, or the speaker must give some kind of background, otherwise the listener can be completely 'lost'. Similarly, readers must have some background knowledge that helps them to understand the text.

Clay talks about a gradient of teacher involvement when introducing a storybook. Maximum support is provided when you read the book to the children. A ***rich introduction*** will be necessary in order to make a challenging book accessible. In a rich introduction, you might read and discuss the title and front cover illustration, discuss illustrations throughout the text, introduce characters by name, discuss significant events within the plot, relate the events to similar events in the children's lives, and so on. A ***short focused introduction*** may be all some children need for the book they are to read. Or you may have little involvement, and provide only a limited introduction, because you believe that the children will read the text with little difficulty. Your involvement in the introduction will vary according to what you know about the children, the book to be read, and the match between them. Again, the art of teaching is knowing how much support to provide, and how much learner responsibility to expect.

Dorn, French and Jones (1998) link the degree of teacher involvement in book introductions with different aspects of the reading program (as shown in figure 4.2).

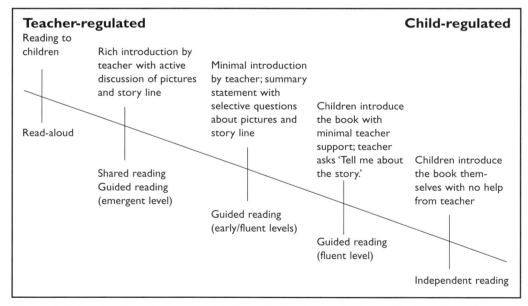

Figure 4.2 Levels of teacher support in introducing books during guided reading (Dorn, French & Jones 1998, p. 44)

Developing the children's purpose for reading

During the introduction, you also help the children themselves to set a purpose for reading. As part of the book introduction, help the children to form questions that they will keep in their minds when they are reading.

> You might say things like:
> *What do you think will happen to ...?*
> *What do you think you will find out?*
> *Does this book make you curious about anything?*
> *What do you want to know about ...?*
> *What do you already know about (the topic)?*
> *What questions do you have about (the topic)?*
> *Do you know any other books about (the topic)?*

When the children form the question themselves, they are much more likely to be engaged in the reading of the text. Holdaway (1979, p. 143) reminds us that 'It is always a good idea to leave children with one or two clear questions which will drive them into the text and serve as a continuing impulse to seek meaning as they read.'

Even though it is sometimes appropriate for you to ask the questions that will set purposes for their reading, the children need the experience of forming their own questions even if the questions result from your interactions with them. With continued experience of this kind, they will eventually ask their own questions when reading text independently. Everything you do will be with the intention of having the children finally take over and do these things independently.

Reading the text

The possibilities

There are two major approaches described in the guided reading literature, as shown in the common overall framework. However, the approaches are not mutually exclusive, and they have different strengths and weaknesses. While I believe that approach *A* generally guides children's reading more effectively (section by section) than approach *B* (reading at own pace), teachers who use their professional knowledge, practical experience and common sense will make the best judgments for the children they are teaching. You need not be restricted by teachers' notes, recipes or orthodoxies of any kind, and can adapt the methodology to maximise the children's ability to read the text independently, with success.

Part 2: Reading the text		
A: 'very' guided reading	B: partly guided reading	Components of A and B
Reading section-by-section	Reading at own rate	Reading first few sections, then reading at own pace.
Teacher guides the independent reading of the text section by section. Brief discussion between each section. Oral reading for real purposes. New predictions made before reading next section.	Children read the text orally, at own pace. Assistance from teacher when necessary. Activities required for early finishers.	Teacher starts guiding the reading section by section, but if the children indicate that they can manage the challenges in the text independently, the teacher encourages them to read on at their own pace.
Most useful when working with a group of children. Overcomes main problems associated with children in groups reading aloud.	Most useful when working with one child. If working with a group, individual children can hear others and 'parrot-read'.	Combines some of the best features of the alternatives described here.

You can guide children through a text section by section; you can get them started by guiding them section by section and then encouraging them to read ahead at their own pace; you can support them as they read at their own pace through the whole text. Adapt the methodology to maximise the children's ability to read the text independently, with success.

> Adapt the methodology to maximise the children's ability to read the text independently, with success.

'Very' guided reading

In the approach we may call 'very guided reading', the children don't read ahead. They read a text section by section, and teachers are therefore able to help them 'talk, think and read' their way through the text in a more guided way than when individual children read at their own pace.

Before each section of text, the children make predictions about what they think is to come. They read the section silently and then discuss it. During the discussion, they read aloud the parts that confirm a prediction, prove a point, answer a question, highlight an interpretation, and so on. Therefore, the oral reading is oral reading for real purposes; it is not 'round robin' oral reading. The section-by-section approach enables the children to keep together, read silently as well as orally, and express the developing meaning *as they read.*

Support for reading section by section

Many writers support the practice of guiding the reading section by section. They have helped us to see the advantages of having children focus on *sections* of text.

Many writers have described guiding the children's reading of *sections* of text. We would do well to remember the excellent work of Russell Stauffer during the 1960s and 1970s. He wrote extensively about 'directed reading-thinking activities', a procedure where children read section by section. Daniel Hittleman (1978) contributed to our understanding when he wrote about 'guided reading-thinking' lessons, and more recently, Jo-Ann Parry (1992) described directed reading-thinking activities and wrote about their effectiveness.

Hittleman made the point that a guided reading lesson is a guided thinking lesson, and he described a procedure that guides children's thinking as they read sections of text. We now commonly use the phrase 'talk, think and read your way through the text' when we refer to guided reading.

While the examples from Stauffer and Hittleman relate mainly to readers in what we would now refer to as the transitional (fluent), self-extending and advanced stages, we can apply the understandings we gain from their work to readers in the emergent and early stages as well.

To guide children's reading section by section, teachers need to be familiar with the texts, and need to determine where they intend to divide the text into sections. In typical simple narratives and personal recounts, you will find an introduction, a series of events, a transition point (usually some form of climax) and a conclusion or resolution. When you identify these sections of the text, they often make ideal sections for guided reading. Quite often, teachers will ask children to make predictions:

- after reading the title and viewing the front cover illustration (and possibly some of the illustrations inside the book)
- after reading the introduction
- after reading one or more subsequent events, and finally
- after reading the event just before the transition or climax.

The procedure is cyclical. For each section of text, the children are asked to

- predict (set purposes)
- read silently or 'whisper read' (process ideas)
- prove (refer to the text to substantiate predictions)

The sample lesson plans in chapter 5 will show the procedure more clearly, but the following paraphrased text from Hittleman (1978) also provides an immediate example.

Title: 'The Mouse and the Lion' (Traditional tale)

- After the introduction (in which children made predictions from the title and front cover illustration):
  Now read the first page and find out what happens.

- After reading the first page:
  What has happened?
  Do you have any idea from this part of the story as to what may happen next?

- After making predictions:
  Now read pages 2 and 3 to find out what does happen.

- After reading pages 2 and 3:
  Were any of you correct in what you thought?
  What do you now think the rest of the story will be about?

In Margaret Mooney's (1994b) notes for guiding the reading of 'How Long is a Piece of String?', the following suggestions are made:

Read pages 5 to 7. What does Max plan to do?

Read pages 8 and 9. Do you think the author is really going to let Max do this? Would you if you were the author?

Obviously, children are taken through the text section by section.

Support materials for the *National Literacy Strategy* in England also indicate that there are benefits in reading sections of text, rather than the whole text 'in one go'. Some of the prompts and questions recommended include:

Read pages …
Read … and find out why … did …

Depree & Iversen (1995) indicate that when children can read silently, 'you may break the text into more manageable units and have them read one or two pages to discover if a particular question has been answered, or to discuss a point.'(p. 34)

Summary

A common procedure, after the book introduction, might be:

1. Each child reads an identified section of text silently.
2. The group discusses the section just read (reflects back). Parts of the text are read orally to support the discussion (there is always a purpose for oral reading).
3. The children make new predictions and read the next section of text. They may be asked to read the next section for specific information, especially when the text is non-fiction.
4. This procedure (predicting, reading silently, discussing and reading orally, making new predictions) may be continued for each section of text, or just long enough to get the children to the point where they can take off on their own.

The children keep setting and refining their purposes for reading, and you keep monitoring their comprehension of the text and their reading behaviours as the reading is in progress. Each child contributes to, and benefits from, the group discussion of each section of text; you do not have individual children reading ahead and without interaction while they're reading. Nevertheless, if the children show that they can probably handle the text independently, then you will often let them read on as you observe and provide help for individuals as needed. Depree & Iversen suggest that the group could even go away to complete reading the book while you work with another group (1995, p. 34). Later, you would bring the group back to discuss their reading.

> When reading section by section, typical questions and prompts might include:
> *Read the introduction (up to page 4) and then tell me …*
> *Now read page 5 quietly with your eyes to find out what happened when …*
> *Read pages 6 to 8 quietly to find out if …*
> *Read on until (main character) gets to the place where … and then we'll talk about what you think is going to happen.*
> *Read on until there's a change that surprises you. What do you think the author will do now?*

'Partly' guided reading
Working with a group

After the book introduction, the children are asked to read the text at their own rate. They are asked to read quietly (or to 'whisper read') but the reading is oral reading so that the teacher can 'listen in' and provide assistance as required.

In the normal classroom, you will usually be working with groups of children. The disadvantages of reading ahead orally include:

- The children read at their own rate and are therefore reading different parts of the text at the same time. You will not be able to listen attentively to all of them at the same time. You will not be able to guide each child's reading as thoroughly and carefully as you can in the alternative procedure which helps children to 'talk, think and read' their way through the text *section by section.*

- At the emergent level in particular, the amount of text on each page is limited, and even though the children might mean to read independently, they tend to 'choral read' (Depree & Iversen 1995, p. 34).

- There is no guarantee that every child is reading the text him or herself. A less confident child may 'listen in' to any of the other children and simply 'parrot read'.

- You can generally only help individual children with problem-solving as they need help; there is little opportunity for the group to work together to solve a problem in the text.

- Children who finish reading earlier are often given 'time fillers' until all children in the group finish reading. (Reading values and attitudes are just as important as reading strategies; we don't want to give time fillers and the negative messages associated with them.)

Working with one child

If you are able to work with one child occasionally (for closer assessment or for more specific one-on-one teaching) then oral reading of the text doesn't lead to the disadvantages listed above. The child will obviously read at his or her own rate without that causing any of the above difficulties either. You are also in a position where you can guide the child *at any time* during the reading; it will not be necessary to work through sections of text. In this case, the child's reading could certainly be 'very' guided.

The interplay between silent and oral reading
What is the place of silent and oral reading in guided reading?

In their excellent book, Fountas & Pinnell (1996) state:

> The goal is for children to read independently and ***silently*** … Children who are just beginning to learn to read are asked to read softly to themselves; soon, they begin to read portions of the text ***silently***. The ultimate goal of guided reading is independent ***silent*** reading. (pp. 4, 8, my emphasis)

In notes for a 'train the trainer' program, Brenda Parkes writes:

> Initially, with emergent and early readers, the independent reading will be of **short pieces of the text**. For example, after they have worked out the title and predicted what might happen in the story, the teacher might ask them to read the first pages **silently**, to confirm their predictions. (my emphasis)

In *Teaching Reading is …* (1981), Sloan and Latham refer to 'audible silent reading' and state that:

> From the time they begin to read, children should be encouraged to read to themselves. The children's first personal reading will frequently be audible but there will be no audience. … As soon as children begin to read stories, they should be encouraged to develop the habit of personal reading for pleasure and for information. Obviously this is best done in a silent mode. (p. 7)

Clearly, we need to work toward silent reading as soon as the children are capable of it. Oral reading will still be important, especially when a child in the group wants to read something to support his or her position, or when it helps an individual child to answer a question.

Many children simply don't realise that reading can be silent

Many children starting school believe that reading is oral because the main demonstrations before coming to school have included parents, and other experienced readers, reading *aloud* to them. They have learned that reading is something you do with your mouth. However, you can help their development towards silent reading.

Make it a game. In shared reading and the language-experience approach, you usually work with the one text over several days. Once it has become familiar, you can ask the children to read a section 'quietly with their eyes'. This can be done in a light-hearted manner. For example, you could say: *Did you know that your eyes and your brain can read? You don't have to use your mouth at all. Let's try it!* They even enjoy covering their mouths with their hands and letting their eyes do the reading. In this way, they learn what you mean when you ask them to 'read with your eyes', and silent reading becomes the automatic behaviour when you make that request.

Many teachers have confirmed this experience: young children in their first year at school can read quietly with their eyes. Some children will continue with what Sloan and Latham call 'audible silent reading', or they may sub-vocalise for some time, but you can model silent reading and request silent reading while waiting for their natural development to occur. There seems to be little current research on the development of silent reading, but experience certainly speaks strongly and indicates that children are capable of silent, personal reading at a very early time in their first year at school.

If you have introduced a book effectively, and matched the text to their ability, many emergent readers will certainly be able to read silently. Obviously, you will allow them to sub-vocalise, or 'whisper read' if they need to. But you will continue to help them with silent reading of familiar shared reading texts, and you will keep referring to silent reading to reinforce the fact that we want them to move towards that behaviour.

Silent reading for emergent readers?

Yes. When children start guided reading, they are not beginning readers. (The main characteristics of the emergent reader are summarised in figure 4.3.) They have already developed the reading behaviours, understandings and attitudes of the beginning reader, and are now entering the emergent stage. (See also pages 16–20.) Many emergent readers can read silently. Certainly, they are often observed reading silently during 'uninterrupted sustained silent reading' time.

Why do we want to develop the habit of silent reading as soon as possible?

Once the children develop the habit of silent reading, each child in the group will have the greatest chance to process the text for him or herself, without hearing all the others reading the text.

There is another reason for preferring silent reading before oral reading in a guided reading session: silent reading is easier than oral reading. To read orally, you have to 'read in your head' first anyway, then you have to employ all the skills and strategies to do with articulation of individual words, and intonation over different sentence patterns. If children have the opportunity to read silently first, their oral reading will be more proficient. Oral reading during the guided reading session should always be for an authentic purpose: to prove a point, to make a comparison, to suggest a motive, to share information, and so on.

Finally, the opportunity to read silently before having to read orally protects the shy child, or the child who may have been put down by others as a result of misreading something. Timid children, or children who lack confidence when reading in front of others, will be much more secure when they have had the opportunity to read silently first.

Emergent readers:

- know how texts work, where a story starts and finishes and which way the print proceeds
- like to look at texts and have texts read to them
- understand that thoughts can be represented by print
- demonstrate reading-like behaviours as they reconstruct texts and role-play reading
- read some known texts, relying heavily on memory and the use of illustrations
- dictate text which they read to others
- respond to and discuss texts, relating what they know about the world and their own experiences to the ideas, events and information in the texts

And they are starting to:

- learn that a text is a consistent way of telling a story or of relating information
- understand that the words convey a constant message
- use illustrations to help them understand the text
- match written words to spoken words
- develop knowledge of sound-letter relationships
- experiment with reading and take risks when reading simple texts
- read much of the familiar print in the classroom and school environment
- express personal views about a character's actions
- retell the sequence of events (or ideas) and are able to make connections between events (or ideas)
- develop an understanding of the concepts of letter, word, sentence
- develop a sight vocabulary of the most commonly used words (can read many in context, and some in isolation)
- recognise and extend alliteration and rhyme
- use semantic cues, syntactic cues, and some graphophonic cues
- read familiar texts with fluency and expression

Figure 4.3 Characteristics of the emergent reader

How will I know how the children are processing the text if I don't hear them read orally?

A counter question could be: *How will you know if a particular child is processing the text when all the children are expected to read orally?* He or she can tune in and listen to any of the other children reading, and simply parrot what they hear.

You don't have to hear the children read all the text orally all the time. You can tell how they are processing the text

- from the points they raise during discussion
- from the predictions they are making

- from the explanations they give when you ask questions such as: *How did you know that? How did you work that out? Where did it tell you that? Does that make sense to you? What do you think the word is?*
- and while they are reading sections orally

Children at the emergent level may be reading books with just a two-word caption on each page, or a sentence or two on each page. Because the text is very short, the discussion following silent reading often includes oral rereading of the text anyway. As children progress through the developmental stages, and the text itself becomes longer, only *parts* of the text will be reread orally. The part a child reads will always be linked to a purpose: to answer specific questions, to support predictions already made, to back up opinions, to challenge another child's comments, and so on.

If you require children to read orally when they first start guided reading at the emergent stage, you must understand your purpose for doing so, and you should allow the children to move towards silent reading as soon as possible.

> **Allow the children to move towards silent reading as soon as possible.**

Some typical questions and prompts for encouraging the interplay between silent and oral reading

When Mooney describes guided reading at the emergent stage, she reminds us to help children learn the sequence of predicting, sampling, confirming and self-correcting. She writes: 'allow children to work through the sequence ***before giving an oral response***.' (1994, p. 21, emphasis added) She suggests many questions and prompts, including the following.

> What do you think the words are going to tell you?
> Look at the text.
> Read it **with your eyes**. [ie silently]
> Does it make sense?
> Were you right? How do you know?
> Now read the text again, or **to me**. [ie. orally now]
>
> (Mooney, 1994, p. 21)

Read to the end of the sentence. [silently]
Now look back at the picture. Why do you think it shows …?
Think what the word could be. [ie in your head, or silently]
Read the sentence with your chosen word.
Did it make sense?
Now tell me what you think the word is. [ie. orally]
Let's read the sentence together and then you will be able to carry on by yourself.

(Mooney, 1994, p. 22)

Mooney then goes on to say: 'As the children become more proficient at integrating sampling, predicting, and confirming strategies and in maintaining meaning, you can guide the children towards coping with **larger chunks of meaning** …' (1994, p. 23, my emphasis)

Typical questions and prompts for oral rereading after silent reading might include:
Read me the part that makes you think that.
Read the part that tells us what the [fox] said to the [gingerbread man].
How do you know …? Read the part that tells you.

Revisiting the text

Revisiting the text will usually include two or three of the following:
- opportunities to reread
- discussion to extend meaning
- exploration of language
- consideration of special features of print or layout
- discussion of the illustrations
- discussion of mood, style, or other characteristics of fiction
- discussion of the information provided in non-fiction

At the early levels, when the books are relatively short (say up to 24 pages), children often prefer to have time to reread the book before they are expected to discuss it. Once books get longer, children won't wish to reread the entire text. They might reread favourite sections, or sections which may not have been fully understood during the first reading.

Rereading: emergent and early readers

The children in the group are given an opportunity to reread the text without interruption. You determine the most appropriate way to handle the rereading during the *previous* part of the session. If the children managed the text easily, you might let them reread it independently. They could do this quietly, or even silently. If they found the text challenging, you might have them read it together, or even have them read along with you. If the rereading is to be oral, the focus should be on smooth, fluent reading and efficient problem-solving. Sometimes, you might have the children work in pairs. Child A reads a page (or section) to Child B, then Child B reads a page (or section) to Child A. With the shorter books at the emergent and early stages, the children could alternate until the book is finished.

Rereading: transitional and self-extending readers

Immediate rereading may no longer be an essential part of the guided reading session. At these levels, the texts are quite long, and rereading a section of the text might be more appropriate. Remember, all children will have opportunities to read the book again on following days. Copies of the book will be placed in the group's borrowing box for this purpose.

Discussion to focus on strategies

You will ask questions that initiate short, specific discussion about strategies the children used to solve challenges during the first reading of the text. This helps the children to articulate the strategies they know and use, and to become more consciously aware of them.

Discussion to extend meaning: emergent and early readers

During the first reading of the text, you helped the emergent and early readers with strategies such as making predictions, confirming or modifying predictions, or making self-corrections. You now use discussion to extend their understanding of the text and to explore aspects such as character, setting, mood and style. You might use open-ended questions to help the children interpret the text, or state what they learned.

Discussion to extend meaning and consider text structure: transitional, self-extending and advanced readers

For transitional (fluent), self-extending and advanced readers, you have already explored character, setting, and so on, during the first reading. You now revisit these aspects of the text, but challenge the children to reach higher levels of comprehension. You will move beyond the levels of literal and inferential comprehension and go into appreciation and critical analysis of the text. It may even be appropriate to look at text structure. In narratives, help them to see how the story is constructed, and have them identify the introduction or orientation, the series of events and complications, and the resolution or conclusion. In non-fiction texts, help them to identify the sections of text that help the author to achieve his or her purposes. For example, in a report, identify the introduction or opening statement which identifies the topic, and the following sections which describe various aspects of the topic. In an argument, identify the author's position, the points made to support that position, and the final restatement of the position. In a discussion, identify the issue, the arguments for and against the issue, and the author's final conclusion. When using non-fiction texts, comment on the use of headings, subheadings, diagrams, and so on.

Exploring language

You can discuss any of the features of the language found in the text. At the early stages, relevant features of print may include alliteration, rhyme, visual spelling patterns, morphemic spelling patterns, high-frequency words, compound words, first person narration, dialogue, onomatopoeia, simple tenses, and so on.

At the later stages, it might be appropriate to discuss abbreviations; similes and metaphors; positive, comparative and superlative forms; analogy; morals; non-inclusive language (eg racist or sexist language); exaggeration; synonyms; antonyms, … the list goes on and on.

Features of print

At the early levels especially, you may revisit the text to comment on the features of print such as:
- use of punctuation to achieve a certain effect
- use of capitals for emphasis
- use of shaped print, words that are s t r e t c h e d or condensed
- aspects of layout

Illustrations

It may be appropriate to have 'a second look' at the illustrations and to discuss with the children how they embellish the text, or how the illustrator has achieved certain effects. Useful teacher reference books include *What's in the Picture?* by Janet Evans (1998), *Pictures on the Page* by Judith Graham (1990) and *Children's Literature in the Elementary School* by C. Huck et al (1993).

It may also be appropriate to consider other visual information, in non-fiction books especially. The text may contain diagrams, flow charts, simple maps, and so on. An excellent reference is *I See What You Mean: Children at Work with Visual Information* by Steve Moline (1995).

Responding to the text

Reader response

It is possible to use many of the guided reading texts to develop and extend reader response. However, it is not necessary to have children respond to every book through art, drama, music, writing, and other forms of expression. The best response to reading is to want to read more.

Most teachers' guides provide excellent ideas for reader response; it is not necessary to include further information about ways of responding to text in this book.

Very often, the 'responding to reading' activities can be done independently, away from the teacher. This can be a time when you are free to work with other reading groups.

Support from parents and other helpers is invaluable. They can help the children working independently while you give your full attention to the teaching group. Some of these independent activities may be set up as learning centres (see chapter 6).

If you don't have another teaching group, and all the children are working at independent activities, this can be a time when you do running records and other forms of individual assessment with particular children.

CHAPTER 5

Sample guided reading lesson plans

Different lesson plan formats

The script format

One format for presenting lesson plans is to write them like 'playscripts' to show how an actual lesson with children proceeded.

Teacher: Have a look at the front cover. The boy's name is Nick, and his father is putting him to bed. What noises do you think Nick might hear in the night?

Sam: He'll hear the cars going by…

Robert: Sometimes I hear a fire truck.

Teacher: Nick might too! What noise would the fire truck make?

Robert: Eee-or, eee-or. *(Several other children chimed in.)*

Teacher: What else might he hear?

Ahmed: He might hear a cat.

Teacher: Yes. And what noise would a cat make?

Ahmed *(and several other children all together):* Mee-ow, mee-ow.

This format provides a record of what actually transpired in one lesson between the teacher and the children. However, it records the details of only **one** lesson, and every time we use a book with children, the procedure will vary in different ways. To get an idea of *all* the possibilities and draw out the *essential* teaching points, teachers need to read through too many of these transcriptions or scripts.

A transcription can only communicate the teacher's response to the way the one group of children read the book. However, different children and different groups will read the text in a variety of ways, including both correct and incorrect readings. A 'composite' format can record several possibilities and allow teachers to get a more complete feeling for the myriad of responses that may come from children.

The 'composite' format

This format distills and recounts the essential 'talking, thinking and reading' that has occurred with many groups of children over considerable time. It shows how you might respond when different children read the text in different ways. It can also show you different ways of interacting with the children when they give correct *or* incorrect responses, as the following example shows.

Text: *What Has Spots*
Literacy Links Plus (Rigby Australia, Kingscourt UK)
LiteracyTree (Rigby USA)
(For full leson plan, see page 105)

This leopard has spots.

4

You might say: *Read page 4 quietly with your eyes to find out what animal has spots.*

Wait until all children in the group have had time to read it and think about it.

If the response is correct, you could say: *Great! Show me the word 'leopard'. How do you know that word is 'leopard'?*

The response could be that child simply looked at the picture and recognised the animal. If so, you could ask questions such as: *How else could you know what animal it was? Have a close look at the word? What other letters do you see?* (We want children to focus on the print as well.)

If the response is incorrect (eg 'tiger'), say: *Listen to 'tiger'.* (You might say the word 'tiger' several times.) *What sound do you hear at the beginning of 'tiger'?* (/t/) *Now, look at the word. Does that word (leopard) start with 't'?*

Discuss with the children. Have them see that the word starts with 'l'.

Ask: *What else could it be?*

If questioning doesn't help the children, TELL them the word 'leopard' and keep reading.

If an incorrect response begins with 'l' (eg 'lion') the children might even say: *I know it's lion, because it starts with 'l'.* In other words, many children even begin to justify their response before you ask them to do so, learning the procedure you follow and anticipating your question even before you ask it. They start to monitor their own strategies.

You could say: *Listen to 'lion'.* (Say the word several times.) *What sound do you hear at the end of 'lion'?* (/n/) *What letter would you expect to see at the end of 'lion'?* ('en') *Now look at the word. Does 'leopard' end with 'n'?*

The children see the mismatch, and realise that they have to self-correct.

Figure 5.1 A composite format which shows various possibilities for the text *What Has Spots?*

Most teachers prefer the composite format because it provides alternatives for them to consider. Some teachers feel that it 'looks' more like an instruction or a prescription that tells them what to say, but when they understand that it is providing 'distilled experience' and alternatives to inform your teaching, they no longer interpret it as a prescription. (Teachers can use a script as a prescription that tells them what to do as well.)

The composite format has been the format used on guided reading handouts for teachers in Australia, England, Indonesia, Northern Ireland, Singapore, and the United States. In every case, the teachers have understood that the format is not a prescription, but a distillation of the experience of working with many children over time.

Which format?

Both formats are used in this book. Some actual transcriptions (or scripts) have been included in the hope that they keep the 'reality' of the lessons with children 'alive'. However, others are written as composite formats in the hope that they bring you broad experience and that they help you find ways of thinking about the essential points and the alternatives.

Sample lesson plans can help you get a feel for how guided reading lessons may proceed, but we repeat that nothing can replace:
- your knowledge of the children (their reading behaviours, understandings and attitudes)
- your knowledge of the texts you are using for guided reading
- your knowledge of the reading process
- your knowledge of what constitutes development in reading
- your knowledge of the total literacy program in your classroom
- your common sense

Other differences

Difference across the developmental stages

It is also important to remember that the guided reading procedure changes as you move through the developmental stages of reading. Some of the steps being suggested in the emergent stage will **not** be appropriate at other stages.

For example, at the emergent stage (especially with books at Reading Recovery levels 1 and 2) you will often read the first one or two pages *to* the children if it helps them to hear and 'tune in' to a repeated syntactic pattern. However, this will rarely be appropriate at the later stages.

Also, at the *emergent* stage, you might guide the children through small sections of the book (page by page, or double page by double page) until they show that they are ready to tackle the text on their own. That will rarely be appropriate beyond the emergent stage, when the sections of text become much longer.

Differences in purpose and procedure

Some of the lesson plans show how teachers include a 'picture chat' through the book as part of the step, 'Introducing the text' (see *What's That Noise?* on page 114, and *Zoo-Looking* on page 135). The lesson plans for the level 1 emergent texts do not include a picture chat as part of the procedure, because books at that earliest level have a perfect picture–text match. If you do a picture chat through those books, you have told the whole story before the children get a chance to read it. (See *A Zoo* on page 100 or *What Has Spots?* on page 105.) Everything we do in the name of guided reading has a purpose; we don't do anything 'as a matter of course'. Unfortunately, in their in-service training, some teachers are learning that a picture chat through the book is an expected procedure for every text at the emergent level. If you are hearing advice like that, you should evaluate it in the light of your own professional knowledge and your own practical experience.

> No procedure or practice is followed 'as a matter of course'.
> Everything we do has a ***purpose***.

Some lesson plans in this book show how teachers have guided the children's independent reading section by section, right through to the end of the book. Other plans show how the teacher has guided the children's independent reading of one or two sections of text, but how he or she has then let the children read on at their own rate once it was established that they could manage the text that way.

The differences shown in the lesson plans reinforce the understanding that there is no one way to do guided reading. As you work your way through the samples, it is important to think of the *purpose* for each interaction between the teacher and the children.

> The differences in the lesson plans reinforce the understanding that there is ***no one way*** to do guided reading.
> They help to remind us that 'the enemy is orthodoxy'.

Over the last two decades, research and experience have greatly increased our understanding of reading and how children learn to read. As a result, our teaching is now more purposeful, or more intentional. In guided reading, we teach with the *intention* that the children will use strategies they know in order to read an unfamiliar text independently – and with success.

The sample lesson plans

Sample lesson plans are provided for the following texts.

Stage	Reading Recovery levels	Titles	Publisher & series
Emergent A	1–2	A Zoo What Has Spots?	RK RK
Emergent B	3–5	Monsters What's That Noise?	HM HM
Early C	6–8	Baby Elephant's Sneeze Taking Photos	MW HM
Early D	9–11	Just Like Grandpa Zoo-Looking	RK SM
Transitional E	12–14	The Fierce Old Woman Who Lived in the Cosy Cave	MW
Transitional F	15–7	Too Much Noise	RK
Self-extending	18–23	The Lonely Giant	RK
Advanced	24+ and beyond RR levels	The Monster of Mirror Mountain	RK

	Australia	United Kingdom	United States
RK	Rigby (Literacy Links)	Kingscourt (Literacy Links)	Rigby (Literacy Tree)
HM	Horwitz Martin (Alphakids)	Horwitz Martin (Alphakids)	Sundance (Alphakids)
MW	Macmillan (Foundations)	Folens (Foundations)	Wright Group (Foundations)
SM	Scholastic (Bookshelf)		Mondo (Book Shop)

GUIDED READING AT THE EMERGENT STAGE

One way of guiding A Zoo

Emergent A	Emergent B	Early C	Early D	Transitional E	Transitional F	Self-extending	Advanced
1–2	3–5	6–8	9–11	12–14	15–17	18–23	24+

Background

During the first six or seven weeks of their first year at school, the children in Carol's classroom were carefully observed as they participated in daily literacy activities. Carol also worked briefly with individual children, and small groups of two or three children, to determine who might be ready to start guided reading. She looked for specific behaviours (such as those suggested on page 89) and finally put five children in a group for their first guided reading lesson.

Carol chose *A Zoo* for this first guided reading lesson, because it is based on a popular topic, and it is a simple caption book with a perfect match between the text and the illustrations. She used the 'very guided' approach through the first few pages, but as soon as the children showed that they were going to manage the text, she let them read on in a 'partly guided' way.

Introducing the text

- Carol encouraged spontaneous discussion of the front cover. She prompted the children with questions such as: *What animals can you see? Where do you see these animals? What do you call a place where these kinds of animals are kept?* She then asked: *How many of you have been to the zoo? What did you see there?*

    Purpose: To engage or 'stir up' the children's semantic knowledge. (You want them to use their knowledge about zoo animals to help them read the book.)

- Carol then continued the discussion with the title page, as the title page has animals that don't appear on the front cover.

    Purpose: To ensure that the children could name each of the animals. Since the children could name all the animals on the front cover and the title page, Carol knew the text would be easy enough for a very first guided reading session. There was no need to do a 'chat through the book'.

- Assessment of the children's ability to name the animals is particularly important for children who have English as a second language. They may know the names of the animals in their own languages, but be unsure about the English vocabulary. If this is the case, you might talk about the animals on the front cover and the title page, or lead a picture chat through the book, with the intention of teaching vocabulary. You might then put the book aside until the next day, when you will review the animals' names using just the front cover and the title page, and then continue with guided reading.

- Carol had determined that the children knew the names of the animals, so she continued with 'tuning them in'. At the very beginning of the emergent stage, Carol often reads just one or two pages to the children.

  Purpose: To get the syntax 'in their ears'.

Note: While we rarely read to the children in guided reading, at this stage there is a definite and legitimate purpose for doing so: we want the children to pick up the syntactic pattern repeated on every page of *A Zoo* (indefinite article + singular noun).

- Now Carol said: *I know you're clever enough to read this on your own. Who would like to read it for us?* The children had just heard Carol read pages 2 and 3, so all were keen to read it for the rest of the group. Carol chose two of the children.

     Purpose: to reinforce the syntactic pattern of the text; to boost confidence and self-esteem; to promote an 'I can do it!' attitude.

Carol knew she had now 'tuned the children in' and set them up for continued successful reading. She had:

- stirred up their relevant semantic knowledge
- ensured that they could name the animals
- helped them to hear the syntactic pattern in the text
- promoted their 'have-a-go' attitude

Carol was now confident that, with continued guidance, they would manage the independent reading of the rest of the text.

Reading the text

Teacher:	Read page 4 quietly with your eyes to find out what other animal we might see at the zoo. *(The children were given time to read the text silently, and then Carol nodded to Justin, as he was obviously very keen to answer.)*
Justin:	A monkey.
Teacher:	Yes Justin! A monkey. Well done. Now, everyone point to the word 'monkey'. How do you know that word is 'monkey'?
Justin:	It starts with 'm'.
Alexis:	And I can see the picture of the monkey. And there's a 'k' right there. *(At this stage, you might expect the children to refer to the initial consonant and the picture, but Alexis was also showing that she can attend to medial letters.)*

Teacher: That's great! You looked at the letters to check. What other animals do you think we might find at the zoo? I want you all to read the rest of the book softly to yourselves. I'll be here to help you if you need me.

The children then read pages 5 to 8, which took less than a minute.

One child, Zach, was clearly puzzled when he tried to read page 8. He asked for help, and the the dialogue continued:

Zach: Does this say lion? *(His tone of voice, and the puzzled look on his face when he pointed to the word, told Carol that he knew it **wasn't** 'lion'.)*

Teacher: Why do you think that word is 'lion'?

Zach: Because the lion is the biggest, and he's at the front. *(Zach's reasoning was logical, but he needed to be directed back to the print.)*

Teacher: Have a look at the word. Now have a look at the title on the front cover.

Zach: Oh, it's ZOO!

Revisiting the text

Rereading

Because Carol had guided the children through the first few pages together, she now provided time for them to reread the text without interruption.

Features of print

Teacher: Turn to page 7 with the picture of the bear. Good. Now, everyone say 'bear' with me three times. *(As the children said 'bear' with Carol, she emphasised the intial /b/ sound.)* What sound do you hear at the beginning of 'bear'?

Justin: /b/

Teacher: Great Justin. Now, who can tell me what letter we use for the /b/ sound in 'bear'?

Zach: 'Bee'.

Teacher: Great! *(Carol wrote a lower case 'b' on chart paper at the easel by her side, then she wrote 'bear' next to it.)*

Andrew: That's like 'Brown Bear, Brown Bear, What do you see?'

Sarah: But it shouldn't have three full stops after it!

Teacher: That's well noticed, Sarah, but when we see three dots together like that it means 'Quick! Turn over! There's something else to come.' When we turn over, we get to the end, where all the animals are back together again. We call the three dots an 'ellipsis'. That's an interesting word, isn't it? *(Young children love 'big' words like ellipsis, and delight in trying to say them. We do not expect them to remember the word, or to have a complete understanding of its use as a punctuation mark at this stage, but a simple explanation is appropriate.)*

The copies of *A Zoo* were put into that group's borrowing box so that they could reread the book at any appropriate time.

Responding to the text

- Before sending the five children to the tables with the collage materials, Carol explained that they were going to make one collage animal each. She assigned each child one animal from the book and explained that the final five animal collages would be stapled together into a big book for later use.

  Purposes: To provide a way for the children to respond to the text. To provide a response that the children could tackle independently.

- When the big book was made the next day, Carol had an ideal opportunity to involve the children in shared writing of a text for their collage animals. She gave them a pattern to follow:

A lazy lion,

a terrible tiger,

…

Purposes: To engage the children in shared writing. To talk about adjectives, or 'describing' words. To use alliteration to reinforce initial consonants.

One way of guiding What Has Spots?

Emergent A	Emergent B	Early C	Early D	Transitional E	Transitional F	Self-extending	Advanced
1–2	3–5	6–8	9–11	12–14	15–17	18–23	24+

Introducing the text

- Before introducing the book, ask the children: *What has spots?* Write a list as they think of things. Show them things you have brought in: material with spots, picture of child with measles, spots on a piece of fruit, tie with spots, and so on.

    Purpose: To engage the children's semantic knowledge.

- Distribute the book. If you have used the question *What has spots?* several times during the discussion, many children now spontaneously read *What has spots?* Discuss the illustrations on the front and back covers. You could talk about the spots on the dog, and the children may be familiar with the story *101 Dalmations*. (Some children may notice that the dalmation's nametag is 'Spot'.)

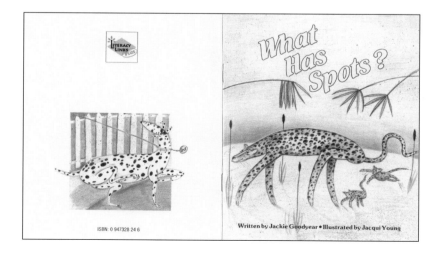

- Ask the children to turn the page.

This clown has spots.   This toadstool has spots.

2   3

- Read pages 2 and 3 *to* the children.

    Purpose: To tune them in to the **syntax** of the repeated sentence pattern on each page; in other words, to get the syntax 'in their ears'.

- Ask: *Who can read pages 2 and 3 for all of us?* Of course they all say they can (they just heard you read it!) so you reread it together. (The children now hear the syntactic structure a second time.)

    Say: *I think you are so clever, some of you could read it by yourself! Who would like to have a go?* Select two or three of the children to read pages 2 and 3 to the group.

    Purpose: To boost confidence, self-esteem, and the attitude that 'We can do this!'

All children hear the repeated sentence structure a few times again, so you have now:

- engaged their relevant semantic knowledge
- tuned them in to the syntactic structure of the sentence on each page
- given them a sense of 'We can do this!'

They are now ready to be guided through independent reading of the rest of the text.

Reading the text

- Ask the children to turn the page.
- **Page 4:** You might say: *Read page 4 with your eyes to find out what animal has spots.* Wait until all children in the group have had time to read it and think about it. If the response is correct, say: *Great! Show me the word 'leopard'. How do you know that word is 'leopard'?* The response could be that child looked at the picture and recognised the animal. If so, ask: *How else could you know what animal it was?* (We want children to focus on the print as well.)

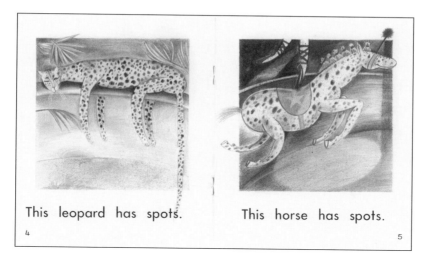

This leopard has spots.

This horse has spots.

If the response is incorrect (eg 'tiger'), say: *Listen to 'tiger'.* (Say the word 'tiger' several times.) Ask: *What sound do you hear at the beginning of 'tiger'? (/t/) Now, look at the word. Does that word* (leopard) *start with 't'?* Discuss with the children and have them see that the word starts with 'l'. Ask: *What else could it be?* If questioning doesn't help the children, TELL them the word 'leopard' and keep reading!

Classroom snapshot

Teacher: Read page 4 quietly and then tell me what animal has spots. *(The children looked up when they had read the text, and the teacher indicated that Peter should answer the question.)*

Peter: *(with glee)*: It's lion. And I know it's lion, because it starts with 'l'.

The teacher often asked the children *How do you know that word is …?* so they had learned that they often had to justify their responses. Peter justified his response even before the teacher asked him to do so. Peter had learned a procedure that the teacher often followed, and he anticipated the teacher's question before it was asked. That is a time to celebrate! Peter shown that he was starting to monitor his own reading, which is exactly what we want him to do. However, in this case, the teacher still had to help Peter look more carefully.

Teacher: Yes Peter, it does start with 'l'. But now, everyone say 'lion' with me three times. *(As the children repeated the word, the teacher emphasised the last sound in the word.)* What sound do you hear at the end of 'lion'? *(/n/)* What letter would you expect to see at the end of 'lion'? *('en')* Now look carefully at the word. Does it end with 'n'?

Peter: Oh. It can't be 'lion'.

Peter saw the mismatch, and realised that he had to self-correct. With the help of the teacher, and the other children, he finally worked out the word and read 'leopard'.

- **Page 5**: Say: *Read page 5 with your eyes to find out what other animal has spots.* Wait for children's response and celebrate if correct ('horse'). If incorrect, you might say: *Point to the word that tells you …* and then continue as above.
- Ask the children to turn the page.

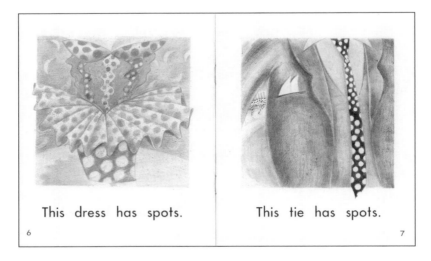

This dress has spots.

This tie has spots.

6

7

- **Pages 6 and 7**: Continue to guide the reading of pages 6 and 7 in the same way.

And this girl has spots.

8

- **Page 8**: When you ask the children to read page 8, they need to notice that the syntactic pattern has been altered by adding 'And …' to the beginning of the sentence. (Note: It is acceptable to begin a sentence with 'and' because it is acceptable to start a sentence with a conjunction. However, it is not acceptable to begin many sentences with 'and' because that would be boring. It is the boring repetition that is unacceptable, not the sentence starting with 'and'.) If a child reads 'This girl has spots', you could say: *Read it for me again, but this time, point to* *the words as you read.* The child will discover the mismatch between the number of words printed on the page and the number of words being read aloud.

Revisiting the text
Rereading

Provide time for the children to reread *What Has Spots?* They could reread the book individually, in pairs, or as a whole group. Pairs may use a form of partner reading. For example, Child A reads a page to Child B, then Child B reads the next page to Child A, and so on.

Features of print

It might be appropriate to comment on any features of print that were raised during the reading of the book, or any features of the book or the illustrations that are relevant.

Responding to the text

- Add some more pages to the story, using the children's ideas. Have the children illustrate the pages and display them as a wall story.
- Suggest that children make a big book with a title such as 'What has stripes?'
- Have children paint some 'spotty' pictures and write captions.

Two ways of guiding Monsters

Emergent A	Emergent B	Early C	Early D	Transitional E	Transitional F	Self-extending	Advanced
1–2	3–5	6–8	9–11	12–14	15–17	18–23	24+

Background

In this class of children in the second half of their first year at school, there were two groups of children reading at the Emergent B band (Reading Recovery levels 3–5). However, one group was more confident that the other, and several of the children were more prepared to 'have a go'. They needed less teacher support to tackle the challenges in the text. The notes under 'Reading the text' show the two different ways in which the teacher guided the children's reading.

Introducing the text

- Before distributing the book, the teacher asked the children what some of their favourite 'monster' books were. He then produced some well-known titles such as Maurice Sendak's *Where The Wild Things Are*, some of the *Monster* books by Mercer Mayer, and *The Very Worst Monster* by Pat Hutchins. He reread *The Very Worst Monster* to the children, and they had a discussion about monsters.

- The teacher then asked: *What would you do, and what would you need, if you were going to dress up as a monster?*

    Purpose: To engage the children's semantic knowledge and stir their imaginations.

- The teacher then gave out copies of the Alphakids book *Monsters*, and asked the children to read the title. They then discussed the illustration on the front cover. The teacher asked: *What have they used to make themselves into monsters?* As the discussion proceeded, the teacher asked more specific questions such as: *What has one of the girls used a sock for? What has one of the boys used long cardboard tubes for?*

Reading the text

I have big eyes
to see everything.

2

I have big ears
to hear everything.

4

Less confident group (greater teacher support provided	More confident group (less teacher support provided)
The teacher read page 2 to the children and then showed them how the word 'everything' is made from two smaller words. This prepared them for the syntactic structure of the sentence on each page, and for meeting the word 'everything' throughout the text. **Teacher:** Now, all point to the word 'everything'. *(Teacher checked that all children were pointing to the correct word, and then wrote 'every - thing' on chart paper on the easel to show how the word was made of two parts.)* **Tony:** It's like 'something'. **Teacher:** Right Tony. Now you all know the word 'everything', and it's in our story a lot today.	The teacher asked the children to turn to pages 2 and 3. They briefly discussed the picture on page 3 and this dialogue followed: **Teacher:** Read page 2 quietly to find out why the girl has big eyes. *(Children read.)* **Shania:** I know why she has big eyes … it's so she can see everything! **Teacher:** Yes! So she can see everything. Let's all read it together. *(Children all read along with the teacher.)* I'm sure you can read the whole story now, right to the end.

Less confident group (greater teacher support provided)	More confident group (less teacher support provided)
Teacher: Turn over and look at the next picture. What has this girl got? **Rachael:** She has big ears! **Teacher:** Wow, she certainly does have big ears. Read page 4 quietly to find out why she has big ears. (The children read quietly.) Who can tell us why she has big ears? (Pointed to Lisa.) **Lisa:** So she can hear everything. **Teacher:** That's right Lisa. Well done! Now, let's all read page 4 out loud together. (This reinforced the basic syntactic structure of the sentence on each page.)	The children continued to read on as the teacher monitored their progress and helped individuals as required.

	Less confident group (greater teacher support provided)	More confident group (less teacher support provided)
Teacher:	Read page 6 to find out what the next monster has. *(The children read.)* What does this monster have?	The children continued to read independently.
Maria:	He's got big teeth!	
Teacher:	Great Maria. Now everyone, point to the word 'teeth'. How do you know that word is 'teeth' Maria?	
Maria:	It starts with 't' and I can see the letters for /t/, /ee/, /th/. *(She pointed to each part as she sounded out.)*	

I have a big nose
to smell everything.

8

Less confident group (greater teacher support provided)	More confident group (less teacher support provided)
Teacher: I'm sure you can read to the end of the story now! The children mainly read silently; two read very quietly.	The children continued to read independently.

Less confident group (greater teacher support provided)	More confident group (less teacher support provided)
The children read the last few pages on their own, and basically finished at the same time. Nick needed help to read 'coming'.	The children continued to read on. Early finishers read the book again, or one of the other monster books available.

Revisiting the text

Less confident group (greater teacher support provided)	More confident group (less teacher support provided)
The children were put into A/B pairs. Child A read one page to Child B, then Child B read the next page to Child A. They alternated through the book, discussing it as they read.	The children in this group were given time to reread the book independently.

Responding to the text

- Materials were available for the children to make monster masks if they chose to do so.
- The teacher reminded the children of the selection of 'monster books' available in the room. He added the guided reading book to the collection and encouraged the children to read or reread any of the books at their leisure.

One way of guiding What's That Noise?

Emergent A	Emergent B	Early C	Early D	Transitional E	Transitional F	Self-extending	Advanced
1–2	3–5	6–8	9–11	12–14	15–17	18–23	24+

Whole-class introductory activity

(20 minutes *before* the guided reading session started)

- During the whole-class introductory activity with her year 1 at the beginning of the school year, Nancy played a listening game with the children. She asked them to close their eyes and rest their heads on folded arms on the desktops. Then she said: *Now I want you to listen to all the sounds you can hear. They might be sounds in our classroom, they might be sounds from the classroom next door, they might be sounds outside. In a little while, we'll talk about all the sounds we hear.*
- As the children described the sounds they heard, Nancy listed them on the chalkboard.
- Nancy asked the children to write the numerals 1 to 10 down the left-hand side of a piece of scrap paper. She then played a tape of different sounds she had recorded (a dog barking, a car driving off, a tap

running, a clock ticking, the sound of herself pretending to snore, the sound of the whistle being blown by the lady on the school crossing, a door slamming shut, and a few other sounds). As she played the sounds, one by one, the children were asked to write down what they heard. They discussed each sound as they proceeded, and the children were thrilled when they had identified the sounds correctly.

Twenty minutes after the whole-class introductory activity, Nancy was sitting the with a guided reading group to read *What's That Noise?*.

Introducing the text

Front cover and title page

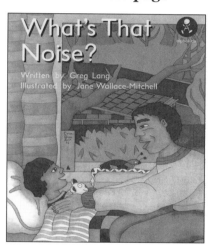
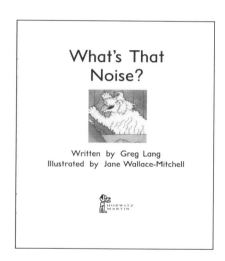

Teacher: What noises did you hear on the tape this morning? *(There was general discussion about the noises they had heard on the tape, and then Nancy showed the children the front cover of the book.)*

Teacher: Have a look at the picture on the front cover. The boy's name is Nick, and his father is putting him to bed. What noises do you think Nick might hear in the night?

Sam: He'll hear the cars going by …

Robert: Sometimes I hear a fire truck.

Teacher: Nick might too! What noise would the fire truck make?

Robert: Eee-or, eee-or. *(Several other children chimed in.)*

Teacher: What else might he hear?

Ahmed: He might heat a cat.

Teacher: Yes. And what noise would a cat make?

Ahmed *(and several other children all together)*: Mee-ow, mee-ow.

Teacher: Let's turn to the title page and read the title together.

Jane *(as soon as she noticed the illustration)*: Look, I knew he was gonig to hear the dog. The dog's going to bark in the middle of the night.

Joel: There might be a burglar!

Kelly: Or a cat outside.

Teacher: OK. Let's read the title together.

All: What's that noise?

Pages 2–3

EE-OW! EE-OW!
'What's that noise?'
asked Nick.
2

'That's a police car
on the freeway,'
said Dad.
3

Teacher: Great! Now turn to pages 2 and 3. There's something making a VERY loud noise. Have a look at the picture. Can you see what it is?

Kelly: A police car!

Teacher: Right. Look it's out on the freeway. *(Nancy used the word 'freeway' knowing that it was a familiar word in their oral vocabulary, but that the children might think the picture was showing just a road. She wrote the word 'freeway' on the small whiteboard next to her, and showed the children how it was made of two parts: 'free' + 'way'.)*

Nancy referred to the print in the illustration, and as she pointed, she read, 'Ee-ow, ee-ow.' She asked all the children to read it with her.

All: 'Ee-ow, ee-ow.'

Teacher: Great! Now, point to the part where it says that in the print at the bottom of the page. *(Nancy looked around to see that everyone was pointing to the right place.)*

Pages 4–9 (picture chat and identification of sounds)

Teacher: Now turn to pages 4 and 5. There's something making another loud noise. Can you see what it is in the picture?

Joel: A red car!

Sam: A red car with its lights on!

Teacher: Right! *(Nancy pointed to the text in the illustration.)* And it goes BRMM BRMM. Can you point to the part where it says that in the print at the bottom of the page? *(Nancy checked visually.)*

BRMM! BRMM!
'What's that noise?'
asked Nick.
4

'That's a car
down the street,'
said Dad.
5

Sam: It says BRMM BRMM in the picture, and it says it down here (*pointing to the text*).

Teacher: Yes. Let's see if it's like that on every page. Turn over to pages 6 and 7.

WOOF! WOOF!
'What's that noise?'
asked Nick.
6

'That's the dog
in the garden,'
said Dad.
7

Kelly: It's a dog making the noise this time.

Robert: Woof! Woof!

Teacher: Can you point to the words for us Robert? (*Robert pointed to the words in the illustration.*) Can you all find those words in the text at the bottom of the page too? (*Visual check.*)

Kelly: It's going to be like that on every page.

Teacher: Let's turn over and check.

Jane: A cat! Meeow. Meeow. (*Several of the children 'chimed in' as they pointed to the words in the illustration or the words in the text.*)

Teacher: Point to the words in the text. Now let's all read them together.

All: Meeow. Meeow.

Teacher: Good. Now you know how this book is going to work. On every double page, there's something else making a noise. The noise it makes is written in the illustration, but it's also written down here *(pointing)* in the text. Now, before we go back and start reading, I want you to put one of these sticky labels on page 9.

Note: Nancy sometimes used removable labels to mark a section of text. The children were familiar with this procedure and anticipated the following instruction.

Reading the text

Teacher: We've already talked our way through the illustrations up to page 9, and we've put a sticky label there. Now I want you to go back to page 2 and read quietly up to page 9 then we'll talk about it. If you finish before someone else, you can go back and read some of it again, or write down any word that gave you trouble.

It took Jane, the quickest reader, just over one minute to read pages 2–9. The others all finished within 15 seconds of Jane. When children read section by section, the 'time gap' between the earliest and latest finishers is not long. Jane was happy to reread parts. When they were all finished, and the discussion started.

Sam: There are noises all night long.

Joel: No wonder Nick can't get to sleep.

Kelly: It's just like that at my house.

Ahmed: Sometimes I hear next door's dog.

Jane: Dogs are okay. It's the cats I hate. They fight outside my house. They make awful noises!

Teacher: Mm, I hate the noise of cats fighting too. Now, everyone turn to page 8, about the cat. *(The children turned to the 'cat' page.)* Joel, can you read pages 8 and 9 for us? *(Joel read aloud.)*

Kelly: Well, it wasn't fighting. It was just stuck in the tree.

Sam: Or it just wanted to come inside.

Teacher: Let's find out what else happened. I want you all to read right to the end to find out if any other noises kept Nick awake. Don't forget to ask me if you need help.

The children all read quietly and independently. Nancy watched for signs that the children might need help, even though they knew they could ask for help at any time. Robert needed help with the baby's noise, 'Wah! Wah!' After they had all finished reading, the discussion continued:

Teacher: Okay. Tell me what other noises kept Nick awake.

Ahmed: The baby was crying.

Robert: Yes, but I didn't think babies made a 'wah' sound. I just know they make lots of noise. That word tricked me.

Sam: Glad we don't have a baby to keep me awake!

Teacher: Were there any other noises that Nick heard?

Robert: The 'click' when his Dad turned the lights off.

Kelly: He was snoring, but he wasn't really asleep.

Teacher: How do you know that?

Kelly: On the last page, look – he opened one eye!

Teacher: Why do you think he did that?

Kelly: He was just tricking his dad. He wasn't really asleep at all.

Teacher: Great! You've all read that very well.

WAH! WAH!
'What's that noise?'
asked Nick.
10

'That's the baby
waking up,'
said Dad.
11

CLICK! CLICK!
'What's that noise?'
asked Nick.
12

'That's me
turning off the lights,'
said Dad.
13

SNORE! SNORE!
'What's that noise?'
asked Mum.
14

'That's Nick sleeping,'
said Dad.
15

Revisiting the text

Teacher: Now, let's have a quick look at each double page. On this side (*pointing to left-hand side*) someone is always asking, 'What's that noise?' On the other side (*pointing to right-hand side*) it's always Dad saying something. So I want you to work in pairs, as you're sitting now. Jane and Robert, you work together. Kelly and Sam, you work together. And Ahmed and Joel.

The children now reread the text, with partners alternating on each double page. Nancy listened as they read aloud, always on the alert to help anyone needing assistance.

Teacher: Let's go through the book and look at all the words for the noises that Nick heard. What do you notice about them?

Robert: They're all in capital letters.

Teacher: Right! And why do you think the author wanted them all in capitals?

Sam: Because they stand out.

Teacher: Uh-huh.

Robert: And it means they're important words. And you have to read them louder.

Teacher: What else tells us how to read them?

Jane: The thing on the end … what's it called? … it tells us to read it louder.

Teacher: Good Jane. Does anyone remember what we call it? Joel?

Joel: It's like a question mark, but that's the question mark there (*pointing*).

Teacher: We call it an exclamation mark. (*Several interjections, as children recognised the name of the punctuation mark.*) And you were right Jane; it tells us to read louder. (*Nancy didn't take it further, but noted that she could plan a 'mini-lesson' on exclamation marks in the next few days.*)

Responding to the text

Nancy discussed and explained the follow-up activities with the children:

- Listen to the audiotape at the listening centre and write a list of the sounds you hear.
- Make a list of the noises you hear when you are in bed at night.
- Write a story about noises in the night.
- Read the books in the 'Noises' box. (Several related books had been collected and placed in a special box. They included *Noisy Nora* by Rosemary Wells, *Mr Noisy* by Richard Heargraves, *Bertie and the Bear* by Pamela Allen, and *What's That Noise? What's That Sound?* by Morris Lurie.)

GUIDED READING AT THE EARLY STAGE

One way of guiding Baby Elephant's Sneeze

Emergent A	Emergent B	Early C	Early D	Transitional E	Transitional F	Self-extending	Advanced
1–2	3–5	6–8	9–11	12–14	15–17	18–23	24+

Introducing the text

- With the children, discuss how you can tell that you are about to sneeze. You might ask questions like: *Does your nose go all fizzy? Do your eyes water? What are some things that make you sneeze?* Just as a matter of interest, you might tell the children that you can't sneeze without your eyes shutting.
- Ask: *What things do people tell you to do to stop sneezing?* (If the children have several remedies to relate, you might write a list on chart paper.)
- Distribute the book. Read the title and discuss the front cover illustration. Ask: *Can you imagine what an elephant's sneeze might be like?* After their response, tell children that this is a story about Baby Elephant's sneeze and what he does to try to stop sneezing.

Reading the text

- Read the title page together. Refer to the illustration and ask: *What happens to Baby Elephant when he sneezes?* (He goes red in the face, his hat flies off, and his trunk shoots out.)

Pages 2–3

- Say: *Read page 2 quietly to find out how Baby Elephant knew a sneeze was coming.* If you get a correct response, celebrate! You might also ask the children to point to the word 'itchy', and ask: *How do you know that word is 'itchy'?*

  Note: It is better to keep the flow of the story going. While they are reading, asking about one or two key words in such a short text would be sufficient. You could focus on other words *after* the reading.

  If a child gives you an incorrect response, you might say: *Look carefully at the word. Could it be what you are saying?* Help the child to read it, or ask the other children in the group for their response.

- Say: *Now read page 3 to find out what his Dad told him to do.* If you get a correct response, celebrate again! If you get an incorrect response, help the children to use the knowledge and understandings they have to read the text correctly.

Pages 4–8

- If the children have been coping with the text well, and you believe that they will be able to meet any further challenges independently, you could now have them read on silently. If necessary, you can provide assistance to individuals.

  When the children have finished reading, you will stimulate discussion by asking questions such as: *What two things did Dad suggest to stop the sneeze? Did they work? Why did Dad tell Baby Elephant to get a tissue?* You can have children refer back to the text to support their statements. Say: *Show me the part that tells you that. Now read it for me.*

Baby Elephant
looked at the light.
"My sneeze is still coming,"
he said.

4

"Hold your nose, Baby Elephant,"
said Dad.
"That will stop the sneeze."

5

Baby Elephant
held his nose.
"My sneeze is still coming,"
he said.

6

"Get a tissue, Baby Elephant.
Get a tissue, quickly!"
said Dad.

7

"Aaaahhhhhh Choooooo!
Aaaahhhhhh Choooooo!"
sneezed Baby Elephant.
"That's better.
My nose is not itchy now,"
he said.

8

Revisiting the text

- Allow time for the children to reread the book for themselves, or to a friend.
- Look at any language features that are appropriate for the group.

  Example 1: You might discuss the final '-y' on the end of 'itchy'. Ask: *What other words do you know that end with '-y' saying the /ee/ sound? There's another one in the story. Can you find it?* Write the words in a list.

  Example 2: You might discuss the use of the exclamation mark on pages 3, 7 and 8.

Responding to the text

- Children can perform the story as a play. You will need to provide the text as a play script for the children to read. For example:

  Baby Elephant: My nose is itchy. A sneeze is coming.

  Dad: Oh, no! Look at the light, Baby Elephant. That will stop the sneeze.

  Narrator: Baby Elephant looked at the light.

  Baby Elephant: My sneeze is still coming.

  There are only three parts, so you could break the guided reading group into three groups (one for each part) or you could let individual children read the parts, and repeat 'the play' several times so that each child participates.
- Have children draw Baby Elephant sneezing and write a story to go with the picture.
- Ask children to find out why we sneeze. They might need to ask the librarian for help.

One way of guiding Taking Photos

Emergent A	Emergent B	Early C	Early D	Transitional E	Transitional F	Self-extending	Advanced
1–2	3–5	6–8	9–11	12–14	15–17	18–23	24+

Introducing the text

- Borrow a school camera, or take your own camera to your classroom. If you have a Polaroid camera, you might take an 'instant' photograph of the children in the guided reading group. As you take the photograph, you could say, CLICK! That will be a good photo! (That line is repeated on most pages in the book.)

- While the photograph is developing, encourage the children to talk about cameras and taking photos, and to share their 'family photo' experiences.

  Purpose: To engage the children's relevant semantic knowledge.

- After you have enjoyed sharing the group photograph, you could write the word 'camera' on a sticky note and attach it to the camera. You could also write the word 'photo' on chart paper and talk about the fact that it is a short form of the word 'photograph'. You might discuss the consonant digraph 'ph' and the sound it makes at the beginning of the word 'photo', especially if you think the 'ph' spelling of the initial /f/ sound is unfamiliar.

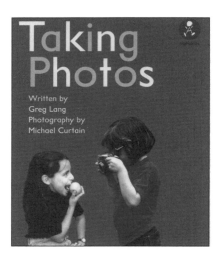

- Distribute the book and ask the children what the girls on the front cover are doing. Tell the children that the girl with the red T-shirt is called Emma. Ask: *What is Emma doing?* Then say: *What about the girl in the black T-shirt? Who do you think she is?* (If the children don't mention that she could be Emma's sister, you might choose to do so.) You could read the title together, or ask if anyone can read it for the rest of the group.

Reading the text

Pages 2–3

- Ask the children to turn to pages 2 and 3. Briefly discuss the picture on page 3. You could say: *Read page 2 quietly to find out what Emma did with her new camera.* Discuss the children's response. You could ask them to point to the word 'family' and you might discuss, very briefly, the fact that 'photos' and 'family' both begin with the /f/ sound.

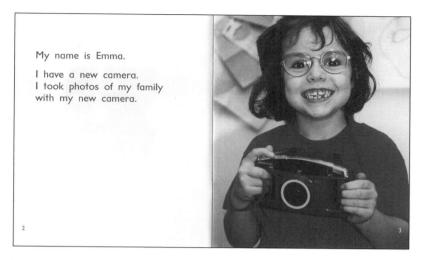

Pages 4–5

* Ask the children to turn over. Their eyes will probably go to the photograph on page 5, so you might want to give them a brief time to discuss it. You could then say: *Read page 4 quietly to find out what is happening.* During discussion of the text, you might make suggestions such as: *Read me the part that tells you where Dad was. Read me the part that tells us what Emma said.*

Pages 6–13

* Pages 6 to 13 follow the same structure as pages 4 and 5. If you believe that the children can now read the rest of the text independently, allow them to read on. Say: *Read pages 6 to 13 to find out what other photos Emma took.* (If you believe that the children still need some help, you might continue to guide them through each of the next three double pages.)

Mum was in the bathroom.
I went up and took her photo.
CLICK!
'That will be a good photo!'
I said.

6   7

My brother was on the phone.
I went up and took his photo.
CLICK!
'That will be a good photo!'
I said.

8   9

My sister was in the yard.
I went up and took her photo.
CLICK!
'That will be a good photo!'
I said.

10

- Since there are only three pages of text, each with the same predictable structure, the children will finish reading them in roughly the
  same time. Discuss the text with them and have them tell you about
  the different people Emma photographed. Have them refer to the text
  to support their answers.

Pages 14–16

- Now let the children read to the end on their own. Discuss the photographs in Emma's album and see if the children can identify the people. They can refer back to the text if necessary.

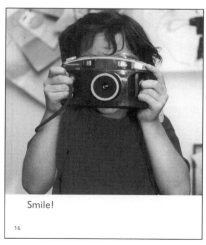

Revisiting the text

- Provide an opportunity for the children to reread the book. Some children may be able to reread independently, but you may need to stay with others.
- You could ask children to find and point to the word 'photo' on page 8. Say the word clearly (perhaps stretching out the first sound) and ask: *What sound do you hear at the beginning of 'photo'? What letters are used to spell the /f/ sound in 'photo'? Can you find another word that starts with 'ph'? Now turn back to page 2. What other words can you find that start with the /f/ sound?*

Responding to the text

Independent activities (away from the teacher) from which children could choose:

- Use a Polaroid camera (for 'instant prints') and take photographs of the children in your group. Make a photo album with captions for each picture. OR
  Cut photographs of people out of old magazines. Make a photo album with captions for each picture.
- Find a book about cameras, or about photography, in your school library. Find out how a camera works.

One way of guiding Just Like Grandpa

Emergent A	Emergent B	Early C	Early D	Transitional E	Transitional F	Self-extending	Advanced
1–2	3–5	6–8	9–11	12–14	15–17	18–23	24+

Introducing the text

The teacher, Richard, had a display of 'grandpa' books, including some that he had shared with the children previously.

Teacher: Let's have a look at these books about grandpas. Are any of your favourites here?

Sarah: My favourite is 'Grandpa's Slippers' because he loved his slippers but Grandma wanted to throw them away.

Maggie: There's 'Grandpa' *(pointing to the John Burningham book)*. That's my favourite.

Jarad: My grandpa looks like him!

Teacher: Let's read it again. *(Richard took the book and read this favourite to the children again.)* Now, let's think about all the things that grandpas like to do. Matthew, what did you want to say?

Matthew: My grandpa likes to sing songs, and he taught me 'Blue Bayou'.

Tai: My grandpa likes to read the newspaper.

When all the children had had an opportunity to contribute to the discussion, Richard introduced the guided reading book:

Teacher: Today we're going to read about a grandpa and his grand-daughter *(holding copy of book up)*. Here's grandpa on the front cover, and here's his grand-daughter. The story is called, 'Just Like Grandpa.' Why do you think it might be called 'Just Like Grandpa'?

Tai: Because she's just like her grandpa. Look *(pointing to front cover illustration)*, she's wearing the same cap as her grandpa.

Jarad: And she's carrying a paint brush just like her grandpa.

Teacher: Well, let's read the story to find out more about why she is just like her grandpa. Let's read the title page together first. *(All read it together.)*

Reading the text

Teacher: Now read page 3 quietly to find out who always says the little girl is just like her grandpa. *(The children read quietly, and when they were all looking up, Richard continued.)* Colin?

Colin: Her mum is always saying it.

Teacher: Great! Can you read the page for us all? *(Colin read the page.)* Now let's look more closely at the illustration. How is the grand-daughter like her grandpa?

Fatima: She's wearing a check shirt just like her grandpa.

Matthew: And she's wearing overalls and orange socks too.

Maggie: What about the brushes and buckets? I think they're going to paint something.

Teacher: Good. Let's start by reading pages 4 and 5 quietly, and then tell me what grandpa likes to eat on his toast.

Note: The question Richard asked provided the help he believed the children needed. His question contained many of the words to be found in the text. When children have just heard the words, they find it easier to identify them in print. Richard could have made the reading task more challenging by saying: *Read page 4 quietly to find out what grandpa likes.*

Teacher: Sarah, what does he like on his toast?

Sarah: Honey. He likes honey on his toast, and so does she.

Teacher: You're right. Do you like honey too?

Sarah: Umm, sometimes.

Teacher: Okay. Now I want you to find out more about what grandpa and his grand-daughter like. Read pages 6 to 13 quietly. I've put a sticker on page 13 so you know where to stop. When you've finished, we'll talk about all the things they like.

Note: Richard uses removable stickers very effectively for this purpose.

My grandpa likes to
draw circles with a stick.

So do I.

8   9

My grandpa likes to
feed the birds.

So do I.

10   11

My grandpa likes to
read his book.

So do I.

12   13

Note: In Richard's classroom, it is established practice to read to the end of the section specified, and not to go past that point. (A removable label certainly helps.) Because the children are grouped according to ability, and because the text is short, they read the text in about the same time.

Therefore, faster readers may finish only seconds ahead of the slower readers. If they do have to wait for others, they know they can look back through the book.

Teacher: Okay. What are the things that grandpa and his grand-daughter liked to do?

Tai: He liked to read books, just like my grandpa, but my grandpa mostly reads the newspaper.

Maggie: But look *(pointing to the picture on pages 12 and 13)*. He isn't reading really. He's gone to sleep!

Tai: Yeh … but he was reading.

Jarad: He liked to draw in the sand with a stick too.

Fatima *(after flipping back through the pages)*: He likes to take the dog for a walk in the park.

Teacher: That's great! You've read that very well. Now, read to the end and find out what else they like to do.

My grandpa likes to cuddle grandma.

14

So do I.

15

I'm just like my grandpa.

16

Matthew: Yuk! Why do they have to finish with cuddling?

Colin: Yeah!

Teacher: Well, I'm sure if I was grandpa, I'd like to cuddle grandma too.

Maggie (*amidst many interjections*)*:* It's okay to cuddle! (*Continued merriment.*)

Revisiting the text

Richard now provided time for the children to reread the book. They had managed the text quite well, so he let them read independently in the reading corner.

Responding to the text

Before sending them off to the reading corner, Richard explained the following activities. They were asked to choose at least one of them.

- Choose some of the other 'grandpa' books to read.
- Draw your own grandpa, or the grandpa you would like to have. Write something about him and the things he likes to do.
- Write a story called 'Just Like Grandma'.

One way of guiding Zoo-Looking

Emergent A	Emergent B	Early C	Early D	Transitional E	Transitional F	Self-extending	Advanced
1–2	3–5	6–8	9–11	12–14	15–17	18–23	24+

Introducing the text

Teacher: Today we're going to read another book by one of your favourite authors, Mem Fox. (*Children make many exclamations of joy.*) I knew you'd be excited to read another one of Mem Fox's books. It's called 'Zoo-Looking' (*holding up the book*). This little girl's name is Flora (*pointing to the little girl on the front cover*). The story tells us about all the animals that Flora saw in the zoo. How many of you have been to the zoo?

Kelly: Me! And I saw a tiger just like that one (*pointing to cover*).

Ben: I've been too. I liked the elephants best.

Francine: I liked the monkeys best. They were chasing each other all over the place!

At this point the teacher, Mary, handed a copy of the book to each child.

Teacher: Let's go through the pictures in the book, and we'll see the animals that Flora saw.

Mary led a picture chat through each double page up to the one before the last. She encouraged the children to name each of the animals and to talk about them briefly. As they did this, Mary used some of the more difficult words from the text as part of her contribution to the discussion. For example, when they came to the double page about the snake, she used the word 'slither', knowing that the word 'slithered' may be difficult for some of the children to read. Occasionally, she would ask the children to point to the word which named the animal they were discussing. For example, when they were discussing the ostrich, she asked them to point to the word 'ostrich'. Then she asked them how they knew that word was 'ostrich'. After some general discussion about zoos, Mary started their independent reading of the text.

One day Flora went to the zoo.

(p.1)

She looked at the giraffe
and the giraffe looked back.

(p.2)

She looked at the panther
with its coat of silky black.

(p.4)

She looked at the tiger
and the tiger looked back.

(p.7)

She looked at the snake
as it slithered through a crack.

(p.8)

She looked at the penguin
and the penguin looked back.

(p.11)

She looked at the monkey
as its baby got a smack.

(p.12)

She looked at the ostrich
and the ostrich looked back.

(p.14)

She looked at the zebra
whose tail went *whack!*

(p.16)

She looked at the koala
and the koala looked back.

(p.19)

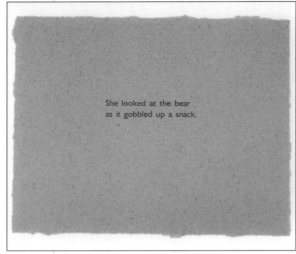

(p.20)

(p.23)

(p.24)

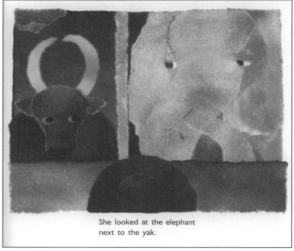

(p.25)

(p.26)

Reading the text

Teacher: Now go back to the beginning and read the story quietly to your-self. I'll be right here if you need my help. When you've all finished, we'll have a talk about the story. If you finish before some of the others, you can reread your favourite pages, or you can flip through the book and decide which is your favourite animal. *(Later, an activity in 'Responding to the text' requires the children to select their favourite animal.)*

The children read the text quietly. (One child still sub-vocalised occasionally, but all the others read silently.) Remember, during the picture chat, they only went up to the second-last double page. The last double page (when Flora looked at her Dad) was left as a surprise for them.

When they had all read to the end of the book, Mary didn't have to open the discussion. There were immediate comments and reactions, including:

Damian: I didn't know they had camels at the zoo.

Belinda: Well, I want to know why the baby monkey got a smack!

Damian: He didn't get a smack, did he?

Belinda: Yes he did.

Teacher: Let's go back to the page about the monkey. Belinda, will you read it for us? *(Belinda read the page.)*

Adrian: So he did get a smack.

Damian: But why? He didn't do anything!

Anthony: Well, it's just, you know … it's just how monkeys play around. It wasn't really a smack. It was just playing.

Belinda: Yes, it was just showing off!

Revisiting the text

Mary asked the children to turn to the double page with the camel, the yak and the elephant. She asked them to read the pages together, and then asked them to identify the rhyming words: *back* and *yak*. She wrote the words side by side, and then asked the children to find other words in the story that rhymed with *back* and *yak*. They found: *black, crack, smack, whack* and *snack*. Mary wrote the words in a vertical list as the children found them. After they read the list together, Mary asked if they knew any other rhyming words to add to the list. They added: *sack, back, pack* and *track*. The 'ck' spelling for the final /k/ sound was discussed, with *yak* being noted as an exception.

Responding to the text

Mary explained the activities listed below, and then allowed time for the children to reread the book independently.

- Draw your favourite zoo animal and write something about it.
- Draw pictures to show

      six slithery snakes
      t............... t .... tigers

- Read another Mem Fox book.
- Find and read some other books about zoos in your school library.

GUIDED READING AT THE TRANSITIONAL STAGE

One way of guiding The Fierce Old Woman Who Lived in the Cosy Cave

Emergent A	Emergent B	Early C	Early D	Transitional E	Transitional F	Self-extending	Advanced
1–2	3–5	6–8	9–11	12–14	15–17	18–23	24+

Introducing the text

- Ask: *What stories do you know where animals talk or act like people?* Children may mention some traditional tales, such as 'The Three Little Pigs'. If they have been fortunate enough to have a rich literature program that has introduced them to Beatrix Potter's animals in *The Tale of Peter Rabbit*, or Rudyard Kipling's animals in the *Just So Stories*, they will mention Flopsy, Mopsy and Cottontail, or the Elephant Child whose 'satiable curiosity' got him into all kinds of trouble. And of course, they will probably mention Wilbur or one of his friends from *Charlotte's Web*.
- Show a copy of the book and tell the children that the story is about a fierce old woman who lives in a cosy cave. She has to stop some animals who want to go into the cave.
- Have the children read the title with you. Discuss the front cover illustration and the illustration on pages 2 and 3. Ask: *What do you think 'fierce' means?* You might ask them to describe the look on the old woman's face on page 3.

Reading the text

- Distribute the books, and ask the children to read pages 2 and 3 quietly to themselves.

- Ask: *What else do you know about the fierce woman now?* If they don't mention that she was fierce when she needed to be, ask them to read the last sentence on page 3 all together. Then ask: *When do you think she would need to be fierce?*

Pages 4 and 5

- Ask the children to turn to pages 4 and 5. Say: *Read pages 4 and 5 to find out why the bear was angry and what he wanted to do.*
- Encourage the children's discussion. Say to one of the children, or the whole group: *Read the part that tells why the bear was angry.* And then: *Read what the bear called out to the fierce old woman.*

Page 6

- Say: *Read page 6 to find out what happened.* When they have finished reading, ask the children to tell you what happened.

Pages 7–16

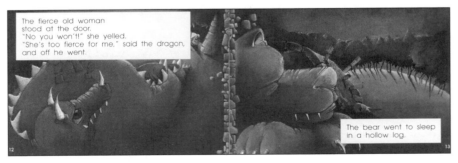

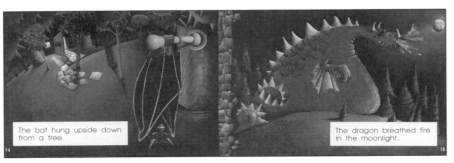

The fierce old woman
went to sleep in her cosy cave.

- Say: *Well, we know what happened to the bear. Now read the rest of the story quietly to yourselves, and then we'll talk about it at the end. If you finish early, reread your favourite part, or start a drawing of the fierce woman.* (The children will finish in roughly the same time, since they are grouped by ability, and the text from pages 7-16 is not that long.)

- After children have finished reading, encourage their spontaneous discussion. If necessary, you might build the following questions into the discussion:

  - *What were the three animals that the fierce woman sent away?*
  - *Did you think the dragon would be scared of the fierce woman? Why/why not?*
  - *What do you think would have happened if the fierce woman had let the bear, the bat and the dragon into her cave?*
  - *What did the animals finally do?*

  Whenever appropriate, say: *Read me the part that tells you that.* (This requires the children to locate specific text and read it orally to support their contention. It also provides you with an opportunity to monitor additional reading behaviours.)

Revisiting the text

- Provide time for the children to reread the story. They might read it quietly on their own, or you could use a form of partner reading. For example, put the children in pairs (one with you if there is an odd number of children). Child A reads a page to Child B, and then Child B reads a page to Child A. They alternate until the book is finished.

- Ask the children to scan the text for other words ending in '-y', like *cosy* (*cosy, angry, furry, scaly*). List the words, and let the children add to the list.

- Ask the children to look for all the words ending in '-ed'. List them (*lived, needed, crashed, stopped, called, yelled, flapped, thundered, breathed*). The list is used in one of the activities below.

Responding to the text

- Have children write some other words that have similar meanings to *fierce*. Suggest that the dictionary might help. Ask: *Which word in your list describes the old woman best?* (The list might include: *bad-tempered, ferocious, savage, wild, violent, cruel,* and others.)
- Children could make a mural or big book version of the story.
- Have children write the story as a playscript and practise it for a performance.
- Ask the children to complete the sheet you have prepared. (You could leave a few blank rows at the bottom for other past tense verbs they wish to add.)

Smallest word	Word + ed	Double letter + ed	Word + d
			lived
need			
	crashed		
stop			
call			
	yelled		
flap			
thunder			
breathe			

One way of guiding Too Much Noise!

Emergent A	Emergent B	Early C	Early D	Transitional E	Transitional F	Self-extending	Advanced
1–2	3–5	6–8	9–11	12–14	15–17	18–23	24+

Background

Jeff, the teacher, identified the four basic sections of this narrative: (1) introduction; (2) series of events; (3) transition; (4) conclusion. He used these sections to structure the guided reading session with a group of seven children in the transitional (fluency) stage.

Introducing the text

Teacher: *(showing the front cover and title page)*: What do you think the story might be about? *(During the discussion, Jeff prompted with questions*

such as: Who do you think this person is? *(pointing to front cover)*
         Who do you think is making all the noise?)

Anthony: Her kids are driving her mad. They must be inside and they're making an awful lot of noise.

Minh: I think it's the kids too, because most mums say we make too much noise.

Shane: Yeah …

Teacher: Any other ideas?

Josh: No. I think it must be the kids too. Maybe something's gone wrong in the house. Maybe the alarm's gone off.

Teacher: Let's read pages 2 to 6 to find out.

Classroom snapshot

When using the same book with a group of children in a school I was visiting, they predicted: 'It's the workmen making the noise.' I wondered what they meant, and when I asked, I discovered that workmen building the major new freeway close to the school had been blasting for weeks. Obviously, the predictions readers make are influenced by their own life experience, and the semantic knowledge they bring to the text. Some predictions come as a surprise, and even though they may not seem fit, they are often seen to be logical when the children are given an opportunity to explain what they mean.

Reading the text

Introduction (pages 2–6)

After reading the introduction, the dialogue continued:

Teacher: Were you right?

Shane: It was the children, but it was the husband too.

Minh: And the cat and the dog.

Maria: Yes, it was all of them. No wonder she was screaming!

(They predicted that the woman's children were making the noise. When they read the introduction, that was confirmed. However, they also had to modify their prediction, as the husband, the cat and the dog were also making the noise.)

Teacher: What do you think the woman is going to do?

Melissa: She's going to scream.

Anthony: Or she's going to get the strap out!

Josh: It's probably not that bad! She'll probably just go to her friend's next door for a cup of coffee.

Suzy: Maybe she'll pack her bags and leave! But I don't really think so. My mum would never do that anyway.

Teacher: Let's read page 8 to see if we find out what she did.

First event (pages 8–10)

After reading:

Teacher: Were you right?

Josh: I was! I knew she would just go to her friend's house. She needed to get out. My mum is always doing that.

Anthony: But she didn't have a cup of coffee!

Josh: She could have! We don't know.

Teacher: Okay. Now look over page 8 again, and read me the part that tells us what the woman's wise friend said.

Melissa: She said, 'I know what to do. Bring your ducks inside.'

Suzy: I don't think that's very wise!

Maria: They'll only make it worse. Why would you take your ducks inside?

Minh: And they'll make a mess! *(Several interjections.)*

Teacher: The woman thought it was a nonsense to bring the ducks inside. Do you think it was a nonsense?

Minh: Yes. They would only make it noisier.

Teacher: Turn over to page 10 and see what happens then.

Dialogue after the children had finished reading page 10:

Teacher: Well, what happened?

Maria: They only made it worse. They quacked all over the place.

Teacher: All point to the word 'quacked'. How do you know it's 'quacked'? *(checking that they were all pointing to the correct word)*

Maria: It starts with 'qu' and it's what all ducks do!

Teacher: Good.

Subsequent events (pages 12–18)

Teacher: Now I want you to read pages 12 to 18 quietly, and then we'll have a talk about it.

Again she went to
her wise friend.

"I know what to do,"
said her friend.
"Bring your chickens
inside, too."

"What a nonsense!"
thought the woman.
But she brought
the chickens inside
anyway.

12

The chickens cackled,
the ducks quacked,
her husband sang,
the children played,
the dog barked,
and the cat meowed.

"TOO MUCH NOISE!"
the woman shouted.
"TOO MUCH NOISE!"
But nobody heard her.

14

Note: Even though this was quiet reading time, by the time some children got to page 16, there were audible remarks. Anthony was heard to say: *Oh no. She's not going back to that woman again!* Shane said: *She is! I don't believe it!* These comments were uttered quietly, so Jeff didn't stop them. In fact, they showed him that the children were engaged with the text, and that they were comprehending it. However, he does not allow the children to start a discussion among themselves at this time; he asks them to wait until they have finished reading the section. The dialogue continued after reading.

Melissa: It just got worse and worse. Now there's more noise than ever! She's not a wise friend at all.

Anthony: She's dumb!

Suzy: But why did the mother keep going back? She's the silly one!

Anthony: She's gotta' get rid of that woman. She should ask someone else.

Transition point in the narrative (page 20)

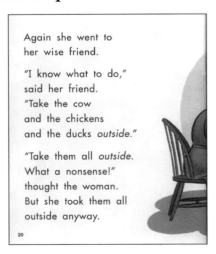

Teacher: OK, let's find out what she does. Read page 20 quietly.

During reading:

Anthony: She's going back to that woman again!

Minh: Shhh!

Maria: But now she's saying to take them all outside. She can't make up her mind.

Anthony: And the mother keeps doing what she says.

Conclusion (pages 22–24)

Teacher: Quick. Read to the end to find out what happens.

As the children finished reading the last page, there were audible sighs and spoken comments as they understood the woman's actions and realised that she really was wise after all.

Out went the cow,
out went the chickens,
and out went the ducks.

Her husband sang,
the children played,
the dog barked,
and the cat meowed.

22

"Ah," said the woman happily.
"What a nice *quiet* house."

Revisiting the text

- In follow-up discussion, Jeff extended their understanding, and they discussed whether or not the wise woman had actually helped the mother or tricked her.
- Jeff provided time for the children to reread the text individually or in pairs (it was their choice).

Responding to the text

Jeff suggested that the children might like to prepare the text for readers theatre.

One way of guiding The Lonely Giant

Emergent A	Emergent B	Early C	Early D	Transitional E	Transitional F	Self-extending	Advanced
1–2	3–5	6–8	9–11	12–14	15–17	18–23	24+

Introducing the text

Related literature

Predictions about giants will be difficult to make from any real-life experience, but the children can be encouraged to make all kinds of predictions from their knowledge of giants in literature. Invite them to discuss stories they know about giants. Hopefully, they will recall the giant in *Jack and the Beanstalk*, and they may recall the favourite line, 'I'll hit you with my bommy-knocker' from *The Hungry Giant*. If they're very lucky, and they've had a good literature program, they may also know *The Selfish Giant* by Oscar Wilde and *The BFG* by Roald Dahl. You might ask: *What are the giants usually like? What are some of the words authors use to describe giants?*

Front and back covers

Ask the children to open the book out so that they can see the whole illustration going across both covers. Encourage spontaneous discussion. You might ask questions such as: *Why do you think the giant is lonely? What sort of a giant do you think he is? What do you think he does all day?*

Title page

Encourage spontaneous discussion, but if necessary, you could ask questions such as: *Who do you think this character is? Where do you think she's going? What might her role be in the story?*

Reading the text

Introduction (pages 2–5)

- You could say: *Read pages 2 to 5 quietly. Find out what it was that the giant wished for, and what it was that puzzled him.* Encourage the children's discussion, and ask them to read what the giant said to himself. Note that the direct speech is printed in colour.

- Ask: *What could the giant do to make the old woman notice him?* Discuss children's ideas before they read the following text.

Series of events (pages 6–13)

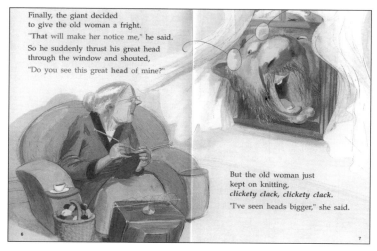

- Say: *Read pages 6 to 13 to find out what the giant did.* The illustrations and the cumulative story structure will support their reading. Provide assistance as necessary. When all the children have read to the end of page 13, discuss the story so far. You might ask questions such as:

What do you think of the old woman? Is the giant the sort of giant you thought he'd be?

Transition point (pages 14–15)

- Say: *Read pages 14 and 15 to find out what the old woman said, and how the giant responded.* Discuss the 'role reversal'. The little old woman is quite sure of herself and the giant is showing himself to be quite gentle and apologetic.
- Ask: *What do you think is going to happen now? How do you think the story will end?*

Conclusion (pages 16–24)

- After the children have made predictions about the ending of the story, ask them to read straight through to the end. Provide support as necessary.

There was a warm woolly hat
for his great big head.

18

There was a warm woolly scarf
for his great big neck.

19

There were warm woolly gloves
for his great big hands,

and there were warm woolly socks
for his great big feet.

20

21

Suddenly, the giant had an idea.
He ran to the woods
and gathered a great pile of firewood,
big enough to last all winter long.

"Now you can be warm, too," he said.

The old woman smiled.
"Thank you very much," she said.

And before long, a beautiful fire
was blazing.

23

Returning to the text

- Discuss the use of coloured print for the direct speech in this text. Use the opportunity to teach or revise conventions about direct speech in print.
- Provide time for the children to reread the text individually. Alternatively, the children could read the story in groups of three: one child could narrate, and the others could read the parts of the old woman and the giant.

Responding to the text

Children could work in pairs to write thank-you letters that the old woman and the giant might write to each other.

One way of guiding The Monster of Mirror Mountain

Emergent A	Emergent B	Early C	Early D	Transitional E	Transitional F	Self-extending	Advanced
1–2	3–5	6–8	9–11	12–14	15–17	18–23	24+

Background

This text has four parts in simple narrative genre: introduction, series of events, climax, and resolution or conclusion. The sections provide perfect 'stopping points'. At each stopping point, you 'reflect back' and then 'predict forward'. During the reflection and discussion, oral reading of parts of the text occurs. Children then make predictions about what might happen next, before they read on.

Preparation

Before distributing the book, fold a piece of paper and use it to 'bind' the last section of the book so that children can't read past page 18. Use a paper clip to hold the folded piece of paper over the last section, ensuring that page 19 is covered.

Introducing the text

Front cover

- Discuss the title and the illustration. You might need to ask questions such as: *Why do you think the men have such surprised or frightened looks on their faces? What do you think might happen in this story?* Provide time for all the children in the group to make predictions and contribute to the discussion, then ask them to read quietly to the end of page 5.

Introduction (pages 2–5)

- After the children have read the introduction, ask: *Who has already rejected their prediction? Why?* Allow time for discussion, then ask: *Who thinks their prediction could still be right? Why?* During discussion, it will be appropriate to say: *Read me the part that makes you think that.*

    Note: It is often appropriate to ask children to read aloud parts of the text that support their predictions, and we will often make that request. However, many predictions are based on inference, so children cannot always find specific text to support their views. Nevertheless, it is appropriate to challenge their views and to expect them to search the text for supporting evidence.

Now you might say: *Mr Talon knows about the monster now. Do you think that will change his plans? How?* If necessary, ask further questions to encourage new predictions, for example: *What do you think he will do now?*

- When there has been ample time to make and discuss predictions, ask the children to read to the end of page 9.

First events (pages 6–9)

- Continue the cycle of independent silent reading, rejecting or accepting predictions during discussion, reading orally to support predictions that still seem probable (or to challenge improbable predictions) and finally, making new predictions.

- If you need to help the children to make new predictions, you might ask questions such as: *Do you think Mr Talon should take the advice of the town's people? Do you really think Mr Talon is brave? Or is he just unaware of the danger? What do you think the people from the town will do? Why?*
- Ask the children to read to the end of page 18.

Continuing events (pages 10–18)

- When all the children have read to the end of page 18, encourage spontaneous discussion. Ask the children to look closely at the illustration. You could ask questions such as: *Can you see Mr Talon? Where is he? What's he saying? Where at the people from the town? What do you think they are thinking? What do you think is going to happen now?*
- When the children have made their predictions, ask them to remove the paper clip and to read on and find out.

"Beware of the monster! Beware of the monster!" the children chanted.

Mr. Talon didn't listen.

As soon as he reached Mirror Mountain he started climbing.

Part way up the mountain there was a clay bank.

It was slippery and hard to climb, but Mr. Talon finally scrambled up. The clay streaked his clothes, and his face looked like he was wearing war paint.

10   11

A little farther up, Mr. Talon reached a patch of brambles and bushes.

The brambles caught on his clothes, and the bushes were full of sticky seed pods that stuck in his hair and on his hat.

Mr. Talon kept climbing, even when he came to a muddy patch that was deeper than he'd expected.

12   13

When he was past the muddy patch, Mr. Talon saw a great wall of rock. He needed his pick and rope, and he had to drive spikes into the rock to use as steps.

Beware of the monster
Beware of the monster
Beware of the monster

Finally Mr. Talon clambered up.

He could hear the distant voices calling, "Beware of the monster! Beware of the monster!"

14   15

Climax and conclusion (pages 19–24)

- Encourage spontaneous responses. Expect children to refer back to the text and read orally the parts which support their views. Discussion usually tells you about the level of the children's comprehension, but if necessary, you should ask questions to check and extend comprehension.

For example: *What did Mr Talon really see? Why did he think it was a monster? What might other climbers have seen?*

Revisiting the text

- Provide time for the children to read the text independently, or to listen to the story on audiotape as they look at the illustrations (or follow the text) in the book.
- You could use sections of the book to talk about features of descriptive text. You could consider the descriptions of Mr Talon after he had slipped on the clay bank (page 11), and after he had walked through the brambles and bushes (page 12).

Responding to the text

- Children could read other 'monster' books from the collection, for example: *Where the Wild Things Are* (Maurice Sendak); *ABC of Monsters* (Deborah Niland); *One Monster After Another* (Mercer Mayer); *There's A Nightmare in My Cupboard* (Mercer Mayer); *Drac and the Gremlin* (Allan Baillie); *The Monsters' Party* (Story Box Level 1)
- Have children compare descriptive passages in the book with descriptive passages from some of the other 'monster' books.
- Children could draw their own monster, and write a description of it

CHAPTER 6

Classroom organisation

with Robyn Platt

The beginning of the year

Getting to know the children

If you are teaching a new group of children, you will need to get to know them in many different ways:

- through listening and watching
- through daily interactions (both during and outside specific literacy times)
- through shared activities with the whole class
- through small group literacy events
- through individual assessments
- through records from the previous year
- through family interviews

Don't forget about important things like sight and hearing. Observe children as they read big books from a reasonable distance, and small books close up. Play listening games to ensure that they can hear you and each other. If you have any doubts, don't hesitate to contact the necessary professional colleagues.

The importance of listening and watching is sometimes overlooked if your workplace puts an emphasis on collection of data about behaviours that can be measured You should plan for active listening and watching. For example, you can plan times for the children to talk about topics such as their families, pets, hobbies, likes and dislikes. If they do this in small groups, you can move among the groups to listen to their conversations and to watch for specific behaviours. You will collect data about language use, but you will also collect data about social and personal behaviours. For example, you will discover which children are natural leaders, and which children are happy to follow. You will discover which children are confident enough to speak out, and which children are going to need encouragement and support. You will also find out which children view themselves as successful, capable learners, and which children lack confidence.

As you learn about the children, they learn about you!

The children need to learn that you have their interests at heart. They need to learn that you are going to support their attempts to learn, and that you appreciate every contribution they make along the way. They need to learn that you have high but realistic expectations, and that you are patient but resolute. You constantly give the message that you *intend* that they will learn.

They need to know that you smile frequently and laugh often. That doesn't mean that you *only* smile and laugh. Sometimes, it will be necessary to make 'the limits' clear and to insist on certain behavioural standards and good manners. As teachers, we will always use good manners ourselves, because children learn what we demonstrate. An influential verse throughout my own teaching career was:

> No printed word or spoken plea
> Can teach young minds what we should be.
> Not all the books on all the shelves,
> But what the teachers are themselves. (*Open Sesame*, p. 230)

Creating a safe emotional climate
No put-downs

We need to build a positive and supportive classroom climate. A climate where the children feel free to explore and experiment, and where put-downs are absolutely banned. It is essential for children to know that they can 'have a go' and that their attempts will be valued. We encourage intellectual risk-taking and help children to understand that mistakes are not only expected, but that they are a necessary part of learning.

Security

We help children to feel secure by being consistent in our interactions and responses with different children. We establish consistent routines so that children know what to do and what the consequences will be if routines are not followed. We have a set of shared 'rights and responsibilities' that are consistently applied for all children.

Belonging

We help children to feel a sense of belonging when they all feel included. Many whole-class activities (such as choral reading, read aloud, singing) and class projects (such as raising money for a social cause) can promote a sense of belonging. We also use inclusive language, or the language of unity: I*t's up to <u>us</u> to work it out together. <u>We</u> need to get that finished by lunch time. Wow – look what you all did when you worked on it together!*

Trust

If children are to be learners in your classroom, they must trust you. They must know that encouragement and support are given as they, the apprentices, work their way towards expertise. They must know that you will respect them an individuals and that you won't embarrass them in front of other people. If you need to discipline a child, it is far better to walk to that child and talk quietly and directly, than to yell across the room. Apart from spoiling the emotional climate, yelling across the room also directs attention to the child's misbehaviour and often results in the child feeling a need to 'perform' in front of the others. As a result, the conflict only escalates.

Developing interpersonal skills

Children need to learn to work with others in positive ways. If children don't have basic interpersonal skills, then these skills need to be demonstrated and taught. Some of the most important skills have to do with a child's ability to 'take turns' and with helping each other to learn.

Taking turns

Some children have difficulty listening and waiting for their turn to contribute to group discussion. They may constantly interject and prevent others from contributing fully. To help a child learn to take turns, Collis and Dalton (1989) recommend the following steps:

- have the child work with a partner rather than a group
- let each child in the pair alternate between 'listener' and 'talker' roles
- when the child learns to take turns with a single partner, let him or her join a small group
- use a physical object (such as a small shell) which has to be passed to each group member as it is his or her turn to talk
- if necessary, have another adult sit with the group to cue each child's turn

Helping each other to learn

Talk with the children about how they can help each other learn. Discuss their need to listen to each other and the ways in which they may respond. Your demonstrations of listening to them, and treating their comments with respect, will show them how to treat each other. Some children also need to learn how to disagree with others, or how to challenge others, while maintaining positive interactions and a friendly classroom. A very useful reference, full of practical ideas, is *Adventures in Thinking* by Joan Dalton (1985).

Creating a supportive physical environment

Ownership

If you involve the children in decisions about how the room is organised, and how the equipment and materials are stored, they will have a sense of ownership that helps them to take responsibility for the running of the room. They will also take more responsibility for tidying the room, returning equipment to the correct places, and keeping everything accessible.

Furniture and space

Organise the classroom furniture in ways which create definite spaces for different kinds of activities. You need a space where the whole class can sit together for shared activities (such as read aloud). You need a 'quiet' area that is separated by bookshelves or display boards from the 'busy' areas. You need work areas with tables and storage facilities. Many professional references provide excellent ideas for planning your classroom; some are listed at the end of this book.

For guided reading, or any other small group work with you, it is a good idea to have a space in a corner of the room, with the children sitting in a U-shape at tables. With three tables placed together, you could have up to eight children sitting around you.

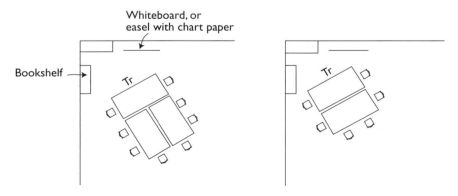

Figure 6.1 Two seating arrangements for guided reading

We sit in an informal circle on the floor with children for many purposes, but for guided reading, it is preferable to have tables and chairs. Sitting on the floor for too long can be uncomfortable, and can lead to 'pins and needles', fidgeting or lack of attention. When children are sitting on chairs, around a table, they are more comfortable, more stable and more attentive. They also have a flat table top for resting their books (which is especially useful when you want them to point to particular features of the book or the print).

Materials and equipment

You need to involve children in decisions about the storage of materials and equipment too. Their personal materials can be kept in tubs or chair-bags or whatever is convenient. Their ideas for storing shared materials are often sensible and practical; after all, they are the ones using the materials.

Routines and procedures

It is essential to develop routines and procedures that help each child to know what is going on, so that they feel secure and so that they can work through the day with a sense of purpose and direction. Talk with the children about your expectations. They can only meet your expectations if they know what they are. Describe and demonstrate processes (how to go about the activities) and outcomes (the results you expect). When there are misunderstandings about the routines or the activities, be prepared to stop the class to explain them, and to clarify your intentions.

Using an activity board for groups working independently

An activity board can be used to show which groups are to complete which required activities, and which activities are optional. The names of the children in each group are written on cards that can be moved when necessary. The required activities are often represented by simple symbols which can also be moved as necessary. Symbols are much easier to use with children in the first year or two of school. Two sample activity boards are shown in figures 6.2 and 6.3.

Independent groups	Required activities for Monday	Optional activities
Damian Francine Fatima George Jarad Margaret Zara	1 Browsing box (independent reading) 2 Word-matching game 3 Nursery rhyme activity 4 Write labels for collage	Poems Listening post Rhyme reading Make a book Choose from the library Personal writing Read to a friend Computer centre: 'The Three Little Pigs' (from Inside Stories) Games Felt board for story map Your choice
Belinda Colin Jarad S Kelly Matthew Tommy	1 Browsing box (independent reading) 2 Nursery rhyme activity 3 Word-matching game 4 Picture cloze	
Adrian Ben Maggie Paul Sarah Tai	1 Browsing box (independent reading) 2 Write labels for collage 3 Picture cloze 4 Word-matching game	
Anthony Beccie Jackie Mike Steve Tilly	1 Browsing box (independent reading) 2 Picture cloze 3 Write labels for collage 4 Nursery rhyme activity	

Figure 6.2 An activity board for year 1

Introducing activities gradually

You will do a lot of whole class work to start with, but gradually introduce group activities and learning centres. The children have to be *taught* how the activities and learning centres work, one at a time. Demonstrate the activities, several times over a few days if necessary, so that you can be sure that the children *know what to do* when they are working independently or in groups away from you.

Required and optional activities

You need to make it clear to the children what you expect them to do when they are working away from you. Some of the activities will be required; others will be optional. The activities you require the children to do may change each day. Others may be on a rotation system (mean-

Independent groups	Required activities for Thursday	Optional activities
Anthony David Fran Joanna Minh Tammy	1 Browsing box (independent reading) 2 Word-matching game 3 Buddy reading 4 Listening post	Poems Book of gimmicks Make a book Choose from the library Personal writing Read to a friend Literature log Computer centre: 'Cinderella' (from Inside Stories) Sound story (with Ms McDonald) Your choice Read another Mem Fox book Games Overhead projector Felt board for story map
Debbie Josh Katie Maria S Mark Nicole	1 Listening post 2 Buddy reading 3 Browsing box (independent reading)0 4 Word-matching game	
Andrew Brendan Libby Maria A Melissa Rodney Scott	1 Browsing box (independent reading) 2 Write labels for collage 3 Picture cloze 4 Word-matching game	
Ari Daniel Jake Kristen Rachel Shane Suzy	1 Buddy reading 2 Make a roll movie (parent helper) 3 Weird and wonderful words 4 Browsing box (independent reading)	

Figure 6.3 An activity board for year 3/4

ing that all children will attempt or complete those activities at some time during the current week); sometimes, other activities will be for certain children only. Different children will take different amounts of time to complete the activities, and some children may not complete the activities but will do as much as they can. The children do not usually rotate at set time intervals. Such practice often cuts learning up into segments, and destroys the good learning habits we are trying to develop. (See Fountas & Pinnell 1996, p. 37 for a more detailed discussion about managing independent activities.)

Some of the activities (both required and optional) might appear on the activity board almost every week, for example: listening post, partner reading (with children from a higher class), choose from the library, personal writing, read to a friend, literature log. Since most classrooms have only one or two computers, computer centre activities *do* appear every week, otherwise children don't get adequate access to the computers.

Sometimes, an activity may appear as a required activity for a particular group, but as an optional activity for the other groups. Some teachers also use pegs or removable labels with the children's names to indicate that certain children are required to complete activities which are 'optional' for others. This can be useful when you know that certain children will benefit from practice on certain activities.

Heterogenous, flexible groups

Groups other than the guided reading groups are heterogenous, and their membership should change periodically, or when necessary. In fact, it is important for the children to have experience working with many different children. You can organise mixed-ability or heterogenous groups so that each group has approximately the same number of children, but variations can occur if certain activities require smaller or larger groups.

Learning Centres
What are they?

Generally speaking, we think of learning centres as those places where equipment is **permanently** set up (such as listening posts, computers, felt boards). When equipment needs to be set up in one place and maintained there permanently, then the children need to be physically present at those centres. However, some equipment is 'portable' and can be used anywhere in the room, and certainly at the children's desks or tables. A centre is not required. This kind of 'portable' equipment would include jig-saw puzzles, some word and sentence matching games, poetry folders, and so on.

It is often appropriate to have temporary centres, where equipment is set up and left in one place for a week or so. For example, you might have a temporary 'games centre' or a temporary 'weird and wonderful words' centre.

We think it is unhelpful to refer to a 'centre' when, in practice, the whole classroom is required for an activity. For example, it can be confusing to refer to a 'writing centre'. How can you have all the children go to a writing centre when you are doing modelled writing or shared writing with the whole class? Obviously, the whole classroom is the writing centre. Even when individual children choose to write, they can do it at a desk. They don't need to go to a centre. You might, however, have a special area where you keep writing paper, pens, pencils, dictionaries, and so on. However, this is a storage area, not a centre.

Similarly, it can be confusing to talk about an 'art/craft centre'. You will have a cupboard or some other convenient place to keep art/craft materials, but a cupboard is not a learning centre. Sometimes, children will use the art/craft materials out in the corridor, or at the 'wet area', or even outside on a fine day.

Most classrooms do not have the space for a large number of centres but the space available, and the storage areas, need careful organisation.

Computer centres

Today, we have computer software which offers educationally valuable programs that use all the capabilities of multimedia presentations. (But beware: some programs still provide only boring skill and drill. Why spend money on this kind of software when a cheap book would have achieved the same low-level learning?)

The good multimedia programs are engaging, and they provide a wealth of literacy activities which have built-in feedback and support systems (such as audio and 'Help' buttons) which help the children to complete activities with success. Many of these are ideal for use in the computer centre. For example, *Sounds Great!* and *Inside Stories* are two comprehensive multimedia programs for the early years of schooling. Both provide stories that act as a springboard for interactive activities designed to develop literacy concepts and skills. The stories can be shown on a large-screen television and used for whole-class shared reading. The on-screen activities provide continual support and feedback, allowing children to work without teacher direction. In both programs, the related print-outs and copy masters provide reinforcement and extension activities away from the computer.

How do your learning centres measure up?

Learning centres are centres for learning. The activities are not busy, fill-in work; they need to have clear educational purposes. Cambourne (1997) provides some very useful guidelines for evaluating learning centre activities in his article "What makes an effective literacy learning activity?', and this article is provided as an appendix.

An established program

The daily literacy block

At the beginning of the school year, it takes several weeks to get routines in place. Gradually, your classroom organisation is refined and your daily literacy block becomes established.

The following sample literacy blocks may help you to see possibilities for organisation and management. The total amount of time you have for your literacy block will vary, depending on the regulations or guidelines provided by your employer. For example, in Victoria, Australia, there is a required 2-hour literacy block every day. In San Diego School District, USA, a three-hour literacy block is mandated. In England, teachers are required to have a 'literacy hour' each day, but most teachers spend at least an hour and a half on literacy.

In the sample literacy blocks described below, the teacher focuses on teaching *reading* skills, strategies, understandings and attitudes during the first three parts of the block, and *writing* skills, strategies, understandings and attitudes during the second three parts.

Obviously, the time you have available for each part will be determined by the time you have available for the entire block.

The sample literacy blocks described below include every strand of your literacy program, including the sustained silent reading time. Some teachers, because of timetabling constraints, personal choice or traditional school practice, have children involved in silent reading at a time outside the literacy block. For example, in some schools, it is traditional practice to have some time devoted to silent reading immediately after every lunch break.

Part 1: Whole-class introductory activity

You normally plan a focus for your whole class introductory activity. The focus may be for one week, but could last for three or four weeks. You might be reading and responding to the picture-story books of Ezra Jack Keats, sharing the humour of tall stories, finding out about the characteristics of fairy tales, considering stereotypes of people of different ages in contemporary fiction, considering the different but important kinds of information gained from fiction and non-fiction books about the same topic, or enjoying free verse poetry. An important aim of the introductory activity is to have the children share in the enjoyment that only books can bring, and to develop a 'reading community' which values reading and seeks the delights of literary experience and shared response. We also aim to introduce the children to as many different authors and illustrators as possible, and to have them experience many different forms of text. We open the world of literature to them, and we broaden their contact with all kinds of information through non-fiction genres.

Fountas and Pinnell remind us that the different components of the literacy program are *not* separate elements. They are 'linked together in two powerful ways: (1) through the oral language that surrounds, supports,

READING FOCUS

1. WHOLE CLASS INTRODUCTION
- weekly focus
- includes READING TO children
- usually includes introductory steps of SHARED READING
- may include shared experience as the starting point for language-experience
- may include a 'mini-lesson' based on previous day's work

2. SMALL GROUP and INDEPENDENT work
Reread familiar texts (could include choral reading; readers theatre; etc)
Language-experience
Shared reading group

GUIDED READING GROUPS
Independent reading
Explicit teaching, or mini-lessons, may result from the above procedures.

eg: text types; linguistic structures and features; features of print; reading strategies (predicting, confirming, and self-correcting using semantic, syntactic and graphophonic information). Retelling; sequencing; innovating on repetitive text structures; predicting consequences when aspect of plot is changed; etc.)

Learning centres
- listening post
- computer
- big book area
- library corner
- reading games
- poems and rhymes
- task cards etc

3. WHOLE CLASS
Sustained silent reading
Share time

WRITING FOCUS

4. WHOLE CLASS
- weekly focus
- often includes modelled writing in front of whole class
- usually includes shared or interactive writing with whole class
- usually includes reading to children
- may include a 'mini-lesson' based on previous day's work
- usually includes a handwriting 'mini-lesson'

5. SMALL GROUP and INDEPENDENT work
- Language-experience
- often includes shared or interactive writing groups
- may include guided writing
- will nearly always include independent writing

Explicit teaching, or 'mini-lessons' may result from the above procedures.
eg: text types; linguistic structures and features; features of print (including punctuation); spelling; handwriting.
Writing of brief stories and recounts about familiar topics; simple procedures (few steps in sequence); personal letters. Experimenting with a range of text types and writing for different purposes (often linked to texts used in shared reading and writing).
Re-reading to reflect on writing and clarify meaning; revision (authorial role).
Editing (secretarial role).

Learning centres
- as above

6. WHOLE CLASS
Share time

Figure 6.4 Sample 2-hour literacy block

and extends all activities, and (2) by the content or topic of focus.' (1996, p.21) The content, or topic of focus, is often evident in the texts chosen for the introductory activity. For example, the introductory activity may introduce texts that help children understand the relationship between the young and the elderly. You might have chosen this focus because it has important links with the current unit of work in social education 'From the cradle to the grave', but during your literacy block, you will use the texts as part of your literature program. You will use them for enjoyment and reader response and to meet the purposes of your literacy program. You will most likely use them for read aloud and for shared reading.

At another time *outside* your literacy block, you may revisit the same texts as resource books for the social education unit. This time, you will use them more for the purpose of discussing the issues and concepts related to the unit (see figure 6.5).

So good texts, related to a topic, can often be the starting point for literacy work and can be used to achieve many of the literacy outcomes required. The content, or topic, links the various components of your literacy program. However, the same texts may also serve an extra purpose. They can promote discussion and assist clarification of many of the issues and concepts related to the 'content units' the children study in social education, science and technology, or health.

Tragically, teachers are often exhorted to 'teach the skills' or 'teach the basics' as if they are divorced from content. Allington & Cunningham state, 'Emphasizing the skill subjects and excluding the knowledge subjects often results in a short-term gain and a long-term deficit.' (1996, p. 44)

Significantly, authors/researchers who have written about the special needs of struggling or 'at-risk' readers, also emphasise that we cannot separate the content from processes and skills. For example, in their book *Readers and Writers with a Difference*, Rhodes and Dudley-Marling write that when struggling readers and writers 'find themselves reading and writing for real reasons (they) come to revalue reading and writing as ways of exploring topics of interest to themselves.' They go on to quote research which has found that 'the broader curricular focus of integrated curriculum positively influences reading and writing development and academic achievement.' (1996, p. 122.)

Let's make some of the links between content and processes/skills more explicit by considering a unit of work. If the unit 'From the cradle to the grave' is being studied in a year 3/4 class, an 'in-built' literature unit may focus on issues to do with aging and the relationships between the young and the elderly. Children will be speaking, listening, reading, writing and thinking for the real reasons to which Rhodes and Dudley-Marling refer.

Week	Texts	Content
1	*Millicent* (Jeannie Baker)	Loneliness in old age; day-dreaming.
	Night Noises (Mem Fox / Terry Denton)	Support of family for 90 year-old who confesses to her great-great-grand-daughter that 'Inside, I'm only four and a half like you.' Loss of hearing.
	The Granny Book (Colin Hawkins)	A funny book of rhyme and annotated illustrations.
	Dreadful David (Sally Odgers and Craig Smith)	David gets up to some of his worst tricks but finds grandmother more than a match.
	My Grandma Lived in Gooligulch (Graeme Base)	A humorous look at an adventurous grandma who is no way a quiet little old lady.
2	*Penny Pollard's Diary* (Robin Klein/Ann James)	Penny Pollard dislikes old people until she meets Mrs Edith Bettany in an old people's home. They become the best of friends.
	Story Makers Part One: Robin Klein (videotape)	Robin Klein as an author. Scenes from *Penny Pollard's Diary* interspersed with Robin Klein describing her craft as a writer.
	Penny Pollard's Diary (audiotape) A selection of Robin Klein books.	
3	*Remember Me* (Margaret Wild / Dee Huxley)	Memory loss. Ellie helps her grandma to remember some important things.
	Wilfred Gordon McDonald Partridge (Mem Fox / Julie Vivas)	Memory loss. Wilfred helps Miss Nancy Alison Delacourt Cooper find her memory.
	'Great-Gran'	Poem by Derek Stuart.
	Song and Dance Man (Karen Ackerman & Stephen Gammell)	For his grandchildren, a warm, wondrous grandpa brings new life to days gone by.
	A Pet for Mrs Arbuckle (Gwenda Smyth/Ann James)	The humorous story of Mrs Emmeline Arbuckle's search for a pet.
	Grandpa's Horses (Kim Lardner)	A tender story of the very special relationship between a little girl and her grandfather.
4	*Waiting for May* (Thyrza Davey)	The authorities want to place Old Alec in an old people's home but Alec has other plans. Desire for independence.
	'He Was …'	Poem by John Cunliffe.
	Nana Upstairs and Nana Downstairs (Tomie De Paola)	Facing death of a loved one.
	Sophie (Mem Fox / Craig Smith)	Facing death of a loved one.
	Annie and the Old One (Miska Miles)	Facing death of a loved one.
5	Review of shared literature Revisiting favourites Comparing styles of writing and linking to authors' purposes	

Figure 6.5 Content unit: 'From the cradle to the grave'
   'Built-in' literature unit: Issues to do with aging; the relationships between the young and the elderly

As already noted, these texts will most likely be used for read aloud or shared reading. When we choose books for guided reading, we choose them because they are at appropriate levels for the groups that we are teaching. The content of the books used for guided reading is rarely a consideration in selection. However, we are aware of the content or topic of the books we intend to use for guided reading, because we have always read them before we use them with the children.

If you know that you will be using the book *Just Like Grandpa* (a book for guided reading at the emergent level) then in the whole-class introductory activity you might choose to read other picture-story books about grandpas such as John Burmingham's *Granpa* and Jeannie Baker's *Grandpa*. Later, when introducing the guided reading book, you can draw on the previous two books in your discussion about grandpas. This will help to activate children's relevant semantic knowledge and 'tune them in' to the text they are about to read.

Ideas for a focus

Mostly, the focus for your whole class introductory activity will be planned ahead of time. However, you should also take advantage of the spontaneous events that occur: the newborn kittens brought to the classroom, the unexpected visitor, the stone that comes smashing through your classroom window when the gardener is mowing the lawn, the book a child brings from home. Chapter 5 of *Read On: A Conference Approach to Reading* has many ideas for introductory activities (Hornsby, Sukarna & Parry 1986).

Part 2: Workshop (small group and independent work)

Organisation and management

It is essential to have well-established routines that all children understand and follow if the 'workshop' part of the literacy block is going to work. The 'workshop' is a very complex time, with small groups and individual children all doing different things at the same time. It is also a busy time for you, the teacher. You will be reminding the children about the day's tasks and your expectations; you will be orchestrating the start of the workshop and 'directing the traffic'; you will be moving throughout the room to supervise children as they get started on their activities. You will then meet your first small group, possibly for a book conference; you will meet possibly another two small groups for guided reading or some other form of instructional reading. Between each group lesson, you will spend a few minutes moving around the room again, checking on the children working at the activities away from you, providing assistance as necessary, and possibly reminding some children of their options and their responsibilities.

Identifying what is to be done, and who is to do it

Activity boards such as those shown earlier in this chapter tell what is to be done (by setting out the required and optional activities). They also tell who is doing what (by identifying which children will be working at the independent activities).

Indicating when and how it is to be done

It is also necessary to make routines or processes clear. The routines described in *Write On* and *Read On* are still relevant. For the reading part of your literacy block, the routines could be based on the flowchart in figure 6.6.

Part 3: Silent reading and share time

Junior classes

After the reading workshop, the whole class comes back together again for silent reading and share time. It is essential for children to have opportunities to select their own reading material at this time. During the whole-class introductory activity, and during the workshop, you introduce or prescribe most of the texts, especially during the first two or three years of schooling. You use authentic texts (texts that are used in the 'real world', texts that are written for real purposes and that have appropriate form and structure for that purpose). You use them because they are going to fulfil real purposes for the reader (related to entertainment, information, and so on) but also because they are going to help you meet the children's needs in terms of their reading development and the skills and strategies they need to learn or practice. You are the best person to make decisions about the texts required for many of the teaching/learning purposes, especially when most of the children in your classroom are still emergent or early readers.

However, it is essential that children have opportunities to select their own reading material as well – and the best way to learn how to choose appropriately is to be allowed to choose. From their very first day at school, all children should have opportunities to choose their own books to read, especially during silent reading time. We can help them with guidelines for making choices, but the final choice should be theirs.

What the children do:

How you will support them:

The children bring their interests, abilities, experiences, ideas, needs, aspirations, hobbies, ...

Whole-class introductory activity
You will plan a focus and use it as a vehicle for:
- sharing enthusiasms about books
- sharing knowledge about authors and illustrators
- reading aloud to children
- presenting the children with many different genres and forms of text
- shared experiences for generation of language
- 'mini-lessons'
- modelling and explaining (demonstrating the thinking that occurs during reading)

The children participate in
Shared activities
- listening and speaking
- reading and viewing
- writing and performing
- language-experience

Reading workshop
Emphasis on
- reading whole texts
- reading books with real' text (ie legitimate genres and forms, from the simplest caption books through to sophisticated fiction and non-fiction forms)
- understanding / comprehension
- strategic reading
- opportunities for first reading of texts to be silent; subsequent oral reading (to support a prediction made, to back up a point, to challenge a different point, to celebrate the sound' of language, etc)
- response (artistic, dramatic, written, etc)
- learning centre activities

Conference groups
- discussion; 'book talks'
- making connections, establishing themes, discussing point of view, etc.
- extending comprehension
- attending to character, plot, setting, style, mood (fiction)
- attending to information (non-fiction)

Teaching groups
- including **GUIDED READING** groups
- focus on strategies
- other instructional procedures
- skills practice

Individuals
- for short, focused teaching and close assessment

Share time
- related reading
- sharing responses
- audience reading

Sharing
Helping children with:
- choral reading
- performance
- debate
- display
- writing
- presentation
- interviewing

Figure 6.6 Suggested routines for the reading part of the literacy block

Beyond the junior classes

Many teachers of children beyond the junior classes prefer to structure the reading session so that time for silent reading is provided before the workshop. Children who are self-extending or advanced readers (or children who are well into the transitional/fluent stage) will often be using the books they read during silent reading time in the workshop as well. These are not the books for guided reading (which are provided as unseen books by the teacher) but the books they are reading for the literature strand of the program, and for other purposes. So the session will be structured in the following way:

- whole-class introductory activity
- sustained silent reading
- workshop (with conference groups, teaching groups, etc)
- share time

It can be advantageous if the children have silent reading time to read their novels and other texts immediately before the workshop, when they will often be used for small group purposes (eg reading conferences, strategy lessons).

Prescription and choice

Prescription and choice are not opposites. For example, even though you need to choose the books to achieve the goals of your introductory activity, that doesn't mean that your choice isn't influenced by the children. Similarly, the children's choices are influenced by you. If you make books come alive in your classroom, you have a strong, positive influence on the choices that children make.

In fact, we could argue that children have no choice if they don't know what the alternatives are. Because you introduce them to many different authors, illustrators, and forms of text, the children have many alternatives in front of them. They therefore have wide choice.

Time for silent reading

Clearly, we must give children time to practice what we want them to do. Ultimately, we want children to be able to read silently and independently, so we must give them time to do that every day. Some children are capable of reading silently at a very early stage in their schooling. Others can be helped to discover that we are able to read 'with our eyes and our brain – we don't have to use our mouths'. (See pages 86–91.) We see many 5-year-olds in their first year at school choosing to read silently during sustained silent reading time. When we observe them, they show us that they can! Other children can be helped towards reading silently if teachers model silent reading, explain it, and have the children practice reading a familiar text silently. However, most teachers of young children, or older struggling readers, seem to prefer oral reading. Is it because they believe they can't monitor children's reading in any other way? When the emphasis is on oral reading, young readers and older struggling readers spend most of their time listening to the other young or struggling readers taking it in turn to read one after the other (see Rhodes & Dudley-Marling 1996; Allington & Cunningham 1996). And yet, what they need most is time on task; time actually *reading*. After all, 'Just plain reading has been shown to improve students' comprehension.' (Pearson 1993, p. 507.)

We practise the skills and strategies of reading by *reading*, not by listening. But of course, listening to expert readers is a different thing. From them, children learn to appreciate all that reading offers. They also witness the mature act of reading, and when that is accompanied by the teacher's explanations and 'out-loud' thinking, there are powerful conditions for learning to read.

If the ultimate aim of your reading program is to help every child become an independent silent reader, then surely there should at least be a balance between oral and silent reading in your program. There will be oral reading during the whole-class introductory activity. There will be considerable oral reading during shared reading and language-experience approach. There will be oral reading during share time. There will also be much oral reading during the writing part of your literacy block. Surely there should be times when silent reading is required. During guided reading especially, there are good reasons for silent 'first reading' of a text, followed by oral reading for a purpose.

Most children seem capable of silent reading within the first six months of their schooling. Some children will still sub-vocalise, and most will sub-vocalise if the text is too difficult for them, or if they are stumped by a challenge in the text. Adults do the same thing. We must allow children to 'whisper read', or sub-vocalise, while that is a normal stage in their development. But we can also help them to discover that reading can be silent, and we can request silent reading when we have a purpose for doing so – even if the outcome is not quite silent. By referring to silent reading, we are reinforcing the notion that it *can* be silent.

Getting started

When do we start working towards sustained, silent reading? From the very first day at school. However, we will obviously need to redefine 'sustained' and 'silent' in the first weeks of the first year at school. On the first day, we will be pleased if each child simply chooses a book, sits with it, and shows an interest in looking through it and responding to the illustrations. At this point, they are usually *not* able to hold their response until a 'community' share time. (As soon as a child turns a page and sees and alligator about to snap at something, he or she will cry with delight, or shriek a warning to 'Watch out!') One of your tasks is to help young children learn to hold their response and to share it during the time when all the others can listen and respond. Before this is possible, it is appropriate to let the children 'read' in small groups and to share their responses with the group. At first, they may 'share' their responses even as they read, but you will help them to discover that, if they keep their responses and share them at the end of the group session, then they will have a more attentive audience and there will be more opportunity for the 'to and fro' of discussion.

Some children, even in the first weeks of school, will be ready to appreciate the benefits of reading quietly on their own, and you should provide a relatively quiet place for them to enjoy their books. Then, at the end of the time for silent reading, you can bring all the children together for whole-class sharing time. It's important for all the children to learn appropriate forms of response in whole-class settings. A whole-class share time also provides sharing opportunities for those children who chose to read quietly on their own.

Share time to celebrate

Share time is a necessary conclusion to every reading session, if only to celebrate the reading that has been done during the session. At the beginning of the year, you may need to organise and guide the children. However, as soon as possible, the children must take the initiative and responsibility for share time.

During share time, the child or group sharing:

- tells about the things which were personally significant
- learns about selecting the most important things to share
- experiences audience response and the attention of peers
- learns how to respond to positive feedback and to criticism
- develops the ability to listen to questions and respond appropriately
- practises audience reading skills and presentation skills
- gains a greater awareness of audience expectations

- encourages others to read certain texts
- develops confidence

During share time, the children in the audience:

- develop the ability to listen
- become more aware of literature and other forms of text
- become more aware of books they wouldn't normally choose themselves
- learn to evaluate recommendations made by those sharing
- learn that reader response varies (others may dislike something you enjoyed)
- develop the ability to evaluate their peers' judgements, opinions and values
- practise questioning skills and learn about the kinds of questions that lead to the most information

> Share time is a necessary conclusion to every reading session. We celebrate the reading that has been done, and we celebrate what we can do.

...epilogue

Guided reading is a powerful teaching/learning procedure, but let's not forget the main aim of a reading program: to help children become independent readers who *choose* to read for many different purposes.

All strands of a balanced literacy program work together to achieve this aim. Guided reading, shared reading and language experience will be important strands of our reading program; we might even refer to them as the *guts* of our program, but a passionate literature strand will be the **heart and soul** of our program, Since we are working with human beings, and not robots, attention to matters of the heart is essential.

We want **all** children to be asking their teachers, parents, and each other:

- Where is Narnia? Do I have to go through a wardrobe?
- How do I get to the place where the wild things are?
- Why can't I grow beanstalks big enough for me to climb up?
- Do little people live under the floorboards of my house and borrow my things when I'm at school?
- Do you think Granma Poss can tell us how to be invisible?

Appendix

What makes an effective literacy learning activity?

(adapted from Set Pamphlet, NZCER and ACER 1997, by Brian Cambourne. Used with permission.)

1. They were linked to other parts of the teaching-learning session (or day)

The activities were not isolated, stand-alone events. They were overtly linked to some other part of the flow of events that occurred each day.

Scenario 1: Four groups, rotating through four learning centres every 15 minutes or so: a cloze activity, a prefixes and suffixes worksheet, a comprehension exercise, sequencing cut-up text. The students see the activities as forms of drill and practice. They don't engage deeply.

Scenario 2: Teacher begins day by reading aloud for 15 minutes. Teacher draws attention to special features of the text (eg author's use of similes). Group activities set up. For example: (A) Revisit the similes in the text and display a criterion chart, 'What makes a simile a simile?' (B) Find examples of similes in other texts, using the criterion chart. (C) Generate a set of similes and share them with the class.

Each of the activities is linked to the other, and all are linked to the teacher-reading episode earlier.

2. They were preceded by explicitly stated (convincing) purposes for engaging in the activity

Successful activities were typically prefaced by teachers explicitly drawing to learners' conscious awareness such things as:

- the reasons for being asked to participate in the activity
- how the activity was linked to the underlying purposes of school learning
- the sub-conscious and/or automatic processes that might be used in the activity

Learners engage more when they understand how the activity fits into the 'big picture'. Explaining the 'big picture' is a form of 'contextualising' or 'situating' the activity. It also reflects the kind of learning that occurs in the everyday world.

3. They involved high degrees of social interaction and cognitive collaboration

They were activities which involved sharing, discussing, arguing, clarifying, explaining, making explicit personal connections, thinking out loud so that others could listen, listening to others think out loud, negotiating meanings and interpretations, jointly interpreting texts, justifying opinions.

4. They coerced learners to use more than one mode of language

These activities required children to talk, listen, read and write.

Scenario 1: Do a sequencing activity alone. (Child uses only one mode of language: silent reading.)

Scenario 2: Put children into small groups and require them to reconstruct the text together. They are to talk about it, and they are to make a list of the textual cues they used to help them do the sequencing. They are to share their list with other groups at sharing time.

5. They coerced learners to draw on more than one subsystem of language

These activities required the children to use semantic, syntactic and graphophonic knowledge in an integrated way. For example, a 'sound search', based on a familiar text, is more effective for helping children learn sound-spelling patterns than isolated activities in a workbook or on a ditto sheet.

6. They encouraged learners to transfer meaning across and/or within different semiotic systems

A semiotic system is simply a system for creating meaning. The predominant semiotic system in human cultures is oral language. Other semiotic systems include art, drama, written language, song, music, sign language, body language, etc.

Literacy learning activities are more effective when they take the meanings that have been constructed using one semiotic system and transfer them into another. Examples: Taking a text that has been read, and converting it into a dramatic performance. Taking a piece of art and describing the meanings in written text. Taking a technical diagram and converting it into written text, or vice versa. Engaging in different forms of paraphrase, eg creating a parody of a well-known form (such as fractured fairy tales).

7. They allowed a range of acceptable responses, that is, there was no one 'correct' answer or response to the activity

Scenario 1: A cloze activity which requires children to provide the word in the original text.

Scenario 2: A cooperative cloze activity which requires children to consider alternative words, and to argue for their acceptance or rejection. Children might even be asked to say which is the 'best' replacement, but to list other possibilities. Everyone's replacement is shared, discussed, defended, justified, negotiated, etc. These processes lead to reflection, intellectual unrest, and modification of one's pool of knowledge and understanding.

8. They were cost efficient and developmentally appropriate

The activities can be applied to texts of different levels of complexity. The processes that children need to draw on can be applied over and over again to different texts of different degrees of complexity and difficulty. *Every* student can attempt a retelling procedure on a developmentally appropriate text; *every* student can attempt to design a blurb for a book they've read during sustained silent reading time, etc.

Further reading

Using literature in the classroom

Daniels, H. 1994. *Literature Circles: Voice and Choice in the Student-Centered Classroom.* York ME: Stenhouse Publishers, and Ontario: Pembroke Publishers Limited.

Fader, D. 1976. *The New Hooked on Books.* New York: Berkely.

Hill, S. & O'Loughlin, J. 1995. *Book Talk: Collaborative Responses to Literature.* Melbourne: Eleanor Curtain Publishing.

Hornsby, D., Sukarna, D & Parry, J. 1986. *Read On: A Conference Approach to Reading.* Portsmouth NH: Heinemann.

Hornsby, D., Ferry, M & Luxford, M. 1989. *Novel Approaches: Using Literature in the Classroom.* Melbourne: Nelson.

Huck, C., Hepler, S & Hickman, J. 1993. *Children's Literature in the Elementary School,* 5th edn.. San Diego: Harcourt Brace Jovanovich.

Nicoll, V & Roberts, V. 1993. *Literature-based Programs: Taking a Closer Look.* Sydney: Primary English Teaching Association.

Perry, A. & Thomas, R. 1992. *Into Books and Beyond: Literature Activities Focusing on Novels.* Melbourne: Oxford University Press.

Roser, N. & Martinez, M. 1995. *Book Talk and Beyond: Children and Teachers Respond to Literature.* Newark: International Reading Association.

Short, K. & Pierce, K. (eds) 1990. *Talking About Books: Creating Literate Communities.* Portsmouth NH: Heinemann.

Sorensen, M. & Lehman, B. 1995. *Teaching with Children's Books: Paths to Literature-based Instruction.* Urbana IL: National Council of Teachers of English.

Veatch, J. 1968. *How to Teach Reading with Children's Books.* Katonah NY: Richard C. Owen.

References

Allington, R. 1983. 'The reading instruction provided to readers of differing reading abilities'. *Elementary School Journal*, May.

Allington, R. 1994. 'What's special about special programs for children who dind learning to read difficult?'. *Journal of Reading Behavior* 26: 1–21.

Allington, R. & Cunningham, P. 1996. *Schools That Work: Where All Children Read and Write*. New York: HarperCollins College Publishers.

Allington, R. & McGill-Franzen, A. 1989. 'School response to reading failure: Chapter 1 and special education students in grades 2, 4 & 8'. *Elementary School Journal* 89: 529–42.

Anderson, R., Wilson, P. & Fielding, L. 1988. 'Growth in reading and how children spend their time outside of school'. *Reading Research Quarterly*. Summer.

Barrs, M. et al. 1988. *Primary Language Record*. London: Inner London Education Authority / Centre for Language in Primary Education (1989. Portsmouth NH: Heinemann.

Butler, Dorothy. 1980. *Babies Need Books*. London: Bodley Head.

Cambourne, B. 1988. *The Whole Story: Natural Learning and the Acquisition of Literacy in the Classroom*. Auckland: Ashton Scholastic.

Cambourne, B. 1997. 'What makes an effective literacy learning activity?' Set pamphlet, New Zealand Council for Educational Research, and Australian Council for Educational Research.

Cassidy, J. & Wenrich, J.K. 1998/99. 'Literacy research and practice: What's hot, and what's not, and why'. *Reading Teacher,* 52, 402–6.

Chambers, A. 1985. *Booktalk*. London: Bodley Head.

Chomsky, C. 1972. 'Stages in language development and reading exposure', *Harvard Educational Review*, 42 (February): 1–33.

Clark, M. 1976. *Young Fluent Readers*. Portsmouth NH: Heinemann.

Clay, M. 1991. *Becoming Literate: The Construction of Inner Control*. Auckland: Heinemann.

Clay, Marie. 1993. *An Observation Survey of Early Literacy Achievement.* Auckland: Heinemann.

Coles, G. 1998. *Reading Lessons: The Debate over Literacy.* NY: Hill & Wang.

Collis, M. & Dalton, J. 1989. *Becoming Responsible Learners: Strategies for Positive Classroom Management.* Hobart: Tasmanian Early Childhood Senior Staff Association.

Cowley, J. 1980, 1990. *Mrs Wishy-washy. New Zealand.* San Diego: The Wright Group.

Dalton, J. 1985. *Adventures in Thinking: Creative Thinking & Co-operative Talk in Small groups.* Melbourne: Nelson ITP.

Daniels, H. 1994. *Literature Circles: Voice and Choice in the Student-centered Classroom.* York ME: Stenhouse Publishers.

Davidson, M., Isherwood, R. & Tucker, E.1989. *Moving On With Big Books.* Gosford NSW: Ashton Scholastic.

Depree, H. & Iversen, S. 1995. *Foundations 1: Teacher's Guide.* Melbourne: Macmillan.

Donaldson, Margaret. 1978. *Children's Minds.* Glasgow: Fontana/Collins.

Dorn, L., French, C & Jones, T. 1998. *Apprenticeship in Literacy: Transitions Across Reading and Writing.* York ME: Stenhouse Publishers.

Durkin, D. 1966. *Children Who Read Early.* NewYork: Teachers College Press, Columbia University.

Education Department of Western Australia. 1997. *Reading Developmental Continuum.* Melbourne: Rigby Heinemann.

Eggleton, J. 1992. *Whole Language Evaluation: Reading, Writing and Spelling for the Middle School.* NZ: Heinemann; Australia: Rigby; Canada: Ginn Publishing.

Evans, J. (ed.) 1998. *What's in the Picture?.* London: Paul Chapman Publishing.

Fader, D. 1976. *The New Hooked On Books.* NewYork: Berkley Publishing Corporation.

Fielding, L. & Pearson, D. 1994. 'Reading comprehension: What works'. *Educational Leadership.* February.

Filby, N., Barnett, B. & Bossart, S. 1982. *Grouping Practices and Their Consequences.* San Francisco: Far West Laboratory for Educational Research and Development.

Fisher, B. & Fisher-Medvic, E. 2000. *Perspectives on Shared Reading: Planning and Practice.* Portsmouth NH: Heinemann.

Fountas, I. & Pinnell, G.S. 1996. *Guided Reading: Good First Teaching for All Children*. Portsmouth NH: Heinemann.

Fox, M. 1996. The place of passion in the development of literacy. Keynote addresss, Early Years of Schooling Conference, Melbourne.

Fractor, J.S., Woodruff, M.C., Martinez, M.G., & Teale, W.H. 1993. 'Let's not miss opportunities to promote voluntary reading: Classroom libraries in the elementary school'. *Reading Teacher* 46: 476–84.

Good, T., & Marshall, S. 1984. 'Do students learn more in heterogeneous or homogeneous groups?' in Peterson, Wilkinson & Hallinan (eds) *The Social Context of Instruction*. New York: Academic Press.

Goodman, K. 1967. 'Reading: A Psycholinguistic Guessing Game'. *Journal of the Reading Specialist* 6: 126–35.

Goodman, K. 1984. 'Unity in reading' in A. Purves & O. Niles eds, *Becoming Readers in a Complex Society*. The 83rd Yearbook of the National Society of the Study of Education, pp. 79-114. Chicago: University of Chicago Press.

Goodman, K. & Goodman, Y. 1979. 'Learning to read is natural' in L. B. Resnick & P. A. Weaver eds, *Theory and Practice of Early Reading*. vol 1: 137–54. Hillsdale NJ: Erlbaum.

Graham, J. 1990. *Pictures on the Page*. Sheffield: National Association for the Teaching of English; Melbourne: Australian Reading Association.

Graves, D. 1984. *A Researcher Learns to Write: Selected Articles and Monographs*. Portsmouth NH: Heinemann.

Hall, M-A. 1976. *Teaching Reading as a Language Experience*, 2nd edn. Columbus OH: Charles E. Merrill.

Harste, J., Woodward, V. & Burke, C. 1984. *Language Stories and Literacy Lessons*. Portsmouth NH: Heinemann.

Harwayne, S. 1992. *Lasting Impressions: Weaving Literature into the Writing Workshop*. Portsmouth NH: Heinemann.

Hickman, J. & Cullinan, B. (eds) 1989. *Children's Literature in the Classroom: Weaving Charlotte's Web*. Norwood MA: Christopher Gordon.

Hiebert, E. H. 1983. 'An examination of ability grouping for reading instruction'. *Reading Research Quarterly* 18: 231–55.

Hiebert, E. H., & Taylor, B. 1994. *Getting Reading Right From the Start: Effective Early Literacy Interventions*. Boston: Allyn & Bacon.

Hittleman, D. 1978. *Developmental Reading: A Psycholinguistic Perspective*. Chicago: Rand McNally College Publishing Company.

Hittleman, D. 1988. *Developmental Reading, K– 8: Teaching from a Whole-language Perspective* 3rd edn. Chicago: Rand McNally College Publishing Company.

Holdaway, D. 1979. *The Foundations of Literacy.* Gosford NSW: Ashton Scholastic.

Holdaway, D. 1980. *Independence in Reading* 2nd edn. Gosford NSW: Ashton Scholastic.

Holdaway, Don. 1990 *Independence in Reading* 3rd edn. Gosford NSW: Ashton Scholastic.

Hornsby, D., Ferry, M. & Luxford, M. 1989. *Novel Approaches: Using literature in the classroom.* Melbourne: Nelson ITP.

Hornsby, D., Sukarna, D. & Parry, J. 1986. *Read On: A Conference Approach to Reading.* Sydney: Horwitz Martin (and Portsmouth NH: Heinemann 1988).

Huck, C. 1989. 'No wider than the heart is wide'.in J. Hickman & B. Cullinan (eds) *Children's Literature in the Classroom: Weaving Charlotte's Web.* Needham Heights MA: Christopher-Gordon: 251-62.

Huck,, C., Hepler, S., & Hickman, J. 1993. *Children's Literature in the Elementary School* 5th edn. San Diego: Harcourt Brace Jovanovich.

Iversen, S. & Reeder, T. 1998. *Organizing for a Literacy Hour: Quality Learning and Teaching Time.* Auckland NZ: Lands End Publishing Ltd; London: Kingscourt; Washington: The Wright Group; Melbourne: Macmillan.

Johnston, P. 1997. *Knowing Literacy: Constructive Literacy Assessment.* York ME: Stenhouse Publishers.

Krashen, S. 1993. *The Power of Reading: Insights from the Research.* Englewood CO: Libraries Unlimited, Inc.

Lo Bianco, J. & Freebody, P. 1997. *Australian Literacies: Informing National Policy on Literacy Education.* Melbourne: Language Australia Publications, for the Commonwealth of Australia.

Luke, A. & Freebody, P. 1999. 'A map of possible practices: further notes on the four resources model,' in *Practically Primary* 4 (2), June.

Lynch, P. 1987. *Using Big Books and Predictable Books.* Gosford NSW: Ashton Scholastic. First published by Scholastic-TAB Publications, Canada 1986.

Meek, M. 1982. *Learning To Read.* London: The Bodley Head.

Meek, M. 1983. *Achieving Literacy.* London: Routledge & Kegan Paul.

Moffett, J. 1987. *Active Voices II.* Portsmouth NH: Heinemann.

Moline, S. 1995. *I See What You Mean: Children at Work with Visual Information.* Melbourne: Longman Australia Pty Ltd.

Mooney, M. 1988. *Developing Life-long Readers.* Wellington: Learning Media

Mooney, M. 1994. *Exploring New Horizons in Guided Reading,* Melbourne: Nelson ITP.

Mooney, M. 1995a. 'Guided reading beyond the primary grades'. *Teaching K–8,* September.

Mooney, M. 1995b. 'Guided reading: The reader in control'. *Teaching K–8,* February.

Moustafa, M. 1997. *Beyond Traditional Phonics: Research Discoveries and Reading Instruction.* Portsmouth NH: Heinemann.

Murdoch, K. & Hornsby, D. 1997. *Planning Curriculum Connections: Whole-school Planning for Integrated Curriculum.* Melbourne: Eleanor Curtain Publishing.

Parkes, B. n.d.. Train the Trainer Booklet, Crystral Lake IL: Rigby.

Parry, J-A. 1992. 'Directed reading-thinking activities' in D. Hornsby, J-A. Parry & D. Sukarna *Teach On: Teaching Strategies for Reading and Writing Workshops.* Melbourne: Phoenix Education; Portsmouth NH: Heinemann.

Pearson, P.D. 1993. 'Teaching and learning to read: A research perspective'. *Language Arts* 70: 502–11.

Pearson, P.D. & Gallagher, M. 1983. 'The instruction of reading comprehension'. *Contemporary Educational Psychology* 8: 317 - 344.

Pinnell, G.S. & Fountas, I.C. 1998. *Word Matters: Teaching Phonics and Spelling in the Reading/Writing Classroom.* Portsmouth NH: Heinemann.

Rhodes, L. & Dudley-Marling, C. 1996. *Readers and Writers with a Difference: A Holistic Approach to Teaching Struggling Readers and Writers* 2nd edn. Portsmouth NH: Heinemann.

Rigg, P. 1989. 'Language experience approach: Reading naturally' in P. Rigg & V. Allen (eds), *When They Don't All Speak English: Integrating the ESL Student into the Regular Classroom.* Urbana IL: National Council of Teachers of English: 65–76

Rigg, P. 1990. 'Using the language experience approach with ESL adults'. *TESL Talk* 29 (1): 188–200.

Rogoff, B. 1990. *Apprenticeship in Thinking: Cognitive Development in Social Contexts.* New York: Oxford University Press.

Rosenblatt, L. 1978. *The Reader, the Text, the Poem.* Carbondale IL: Southern Illinois University Press.

Rosenblatt, L. 1985. 'Viewpoints: Transaction versus interaction – a terminological rescue operation'. *Research in the Teaching of English* 19: 96–107.